Open Learning

Microsoft Word for Windows

Version 2

Sten Bonnedurar
12/9/94

Open Learning

Microsoft
Word for Windows
Version 2

G G Skinner & E M Prentice

PITMAN PUBLISHING
128 Long Acre, London, WC2E 9AN
A Division of Longman Group UK Limited

First published in Great Britain 1993
Reprinted 1993

British Library Cataloguing-in-Publication Data
A catalogue record for this book is available
from the British Library

ISBN 0 273 03809 5

Printed in England by Clays Ltd, St Ives plc

Acknowledgements

Microsoft Word for Windows, MS-DOS and Windows are registered trademarks of Microsoft Corporation.
IBM is a registered trademark of International Business Machines Corporation.

Contents

Introduction

Overview

Microsoft Word for Windows version 2 is a word processing package which runs on an IBM PC-compatible microcomputer. It requires Microsoft Windows (version 3.0 at least) to be installed on your machine.

Using this book

This book is intended for the use of anyone who wishes to learn Word for Windows version 2, with little or no additional support. Each unit can be used independently, so that you can practise any particular aspect of the software without necessarily working through all the units which precede it.

Most of the activities are based on realistic business documents so that you will learn the standard layout and design of these documents while acquiring operating knowledge and skills.

Each free-standing unit consists of existing skills, some new skills, activities and instructions. Once you have read and understood each group of instructions, you will be able to undertake the activity which goes with them. The units also contain suggestions for further use of the techniques included, and solutions to the problems which you may encounter.

If you want to use a particular unit, then you should first check that you have already mastered the existing skills you need for it.

Unit X
Overview
Existing skills
New skills
Numbered instructions
Activities
Further uses
Problem solving

Operation

Word for Windows is operated through menus which are selected with a mouse pointer in one of the following ways:

• Menus

Using your mouse, point at one of the options on the menu bar at the top of the screen and click the left mouse button. The appropriate pull-down menu will be displayed. You can then make selections from the menu by pointing at the option and clicking the left mouse button.

• Toolbar and ribbon

All the available options can be selected through the menu. In addition, some of the options that are used most often have special buttons displayed on screen on the toolbar and ribbon. Clicking the mouse pointer on these buttons gives the option immediately, rather than going through menus.

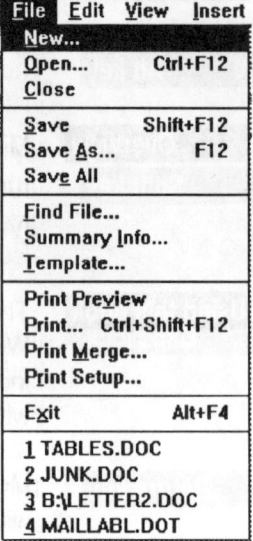

Toolbar Ribbon Menu bar Ruler

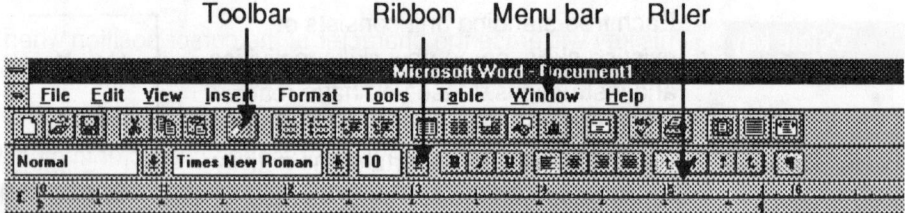

• Keyboard

Although a mouse is an essential requirement for using all Windows-based software, you can carry out many operations with the keyboard. You can pull down the menus by *holding down* the **Alt** key, at the left-hand side of the space bar on your keyboard and then pressing the underlined letter for any of the menus on the menu bar.

Once a pull-down menu is displayed, you can select an option by typing its underlined letter, or highlighting it with the cursor (using the cursor control arrow keys) and pressing **Return**.

Using keys

Function keys
The function keys should be found above or to the left of the main keyboard, marked **F1** to **F10**, or **F12**, depending on your keyboard. Some functions are listed on menus as 'short cut keys'.

Alt key
The **Alt** (Alternate) key can used to access the menus if you have no mouse installed. Hold it down and press the first letter of the menu you want.

Shift key
If the **Shift** key is held down and used with any of the alphabetic keys, this will give you upper case, in the same way as a conventional typewriter. It can also be used in conjunction with the function keys (like **Ctrl** and **Alt**).

Caps lock
If you need a number of characters in upper case, pressing the **Caps lock** key on will enable you to type them without having to hold down the **Shift** key.

Return key
The **Return** key is used to complete a menu entry as well as to move the cursor to a new line. The **Enter** key on the numeric keypad is identical in effect and can be used as an alternative to it.

Delete key
This key will erase the character at the cursor position when pressed; if held down it will automatically carry on erasing.

Backspace key
The **Backspace** delete key will erase the character immediately to the left of the cursor position; if held down it will automatically carry on erasing.

Insert key
The **Insert** key, when pressed, selects INSERT MODE (you can insert additional text without affecting what is there already) and TYPE MODE (text typed replaces existing text).

Cursor keys
The cursor arrow keys on the numeric keypad to the right of the main keyboard (and repeated between the numeric and main keyboards on an extended keyboard) move the cursor position in the direction indicated. They are also used to move the cursor in menus. The cursor marker on the screen shows your current typing position.

Using the mouse

Mouse operation is an integral feature of using any Windows application. If you move the mouse, you will see the pointer move over the screen.

Using the mouse requires you to perform three distinct actions:

• Clicking

Point at something, press and quickly release the left mouse button. This is usually used for selection and applies to windows, icons, buttons, menus and positioning the text cursor.

• Double-clicking

Point at something and click twice in rapid succession. A *light* touch on the mouse button will allow faster clicking.

• Dragging

Point at something, depress the left mouse button and hold it down while moving the mouse. Boxes and windows can be dragged by pointing at their title bar. Program icons can also be dragged within their windows in the Program Manager screen. You may do this by mistake, when trying to start up an application with double clicking.

Window sizing

It is always possible to change the size of a window. At the right-hand end of the title bar there are two square **buttons**.

Maximise

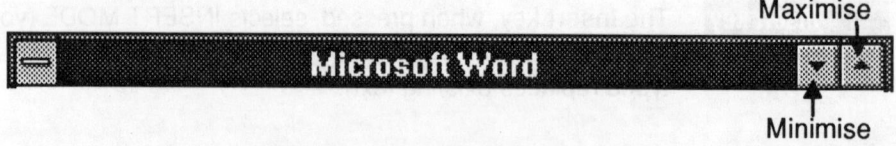

Minimise

When you click on the **maximise** button the window will expand to fill the whole screen. A button with two arrows appears under the maximise button. This is the **restore** button. Click it to restore the window to its original size and position.

When you click on the **minimise** button the whole window collapses to a small box. To restore, click on it and then click **Restore** on the little menu which appears.

Preparing for Word for Windows

Overview   Word for Windows is a very powerful word processing program, which is capable of being set up to work in a number of different ways. Before you use Units 1 - 21, you need to set up Word for Windows in a way which will make it easier for you to use the material.

All you have to do is to follow the procedure given in this unit very carefully. It is not necessary to understand all the steps you are taking. Most of them will become clear to you as you work through the material.

Important   **1** If you have any problems in your preparation, then the best thing to do is to ask a more experienced friend to do it for you.

     2 Throughout this material, it is assumed that you are using a machine on which Windows version 3 and Word for Windows version 2 have been installed.

1 Installation

1 Check that Windows version 3 or higher is installed on your machine and that you have at least 8 Mb of free space on your hard disk. For a full installation of all Word for Windows' options, including the Online Lessons and Text Conversions, you will need 15 Mb free space.

2 Follow the instructions to install Word for Windows given on the Jump Start card provided with the software, accepting any options given to you about disk drives and directories.

3 If a message is displayed telling you that you have insufficient space to install all the options you have chosen, then use the dialog box below to limit the options you will install. You will not need the Online Lessons or the Text Conversions/Graphics Filters to use the Units.

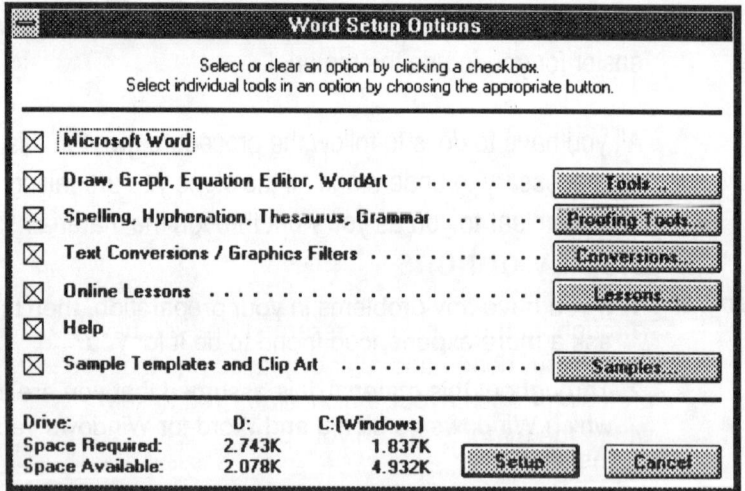

2 Loading Word for Windows

1 Start up Windows to display the Program Manager screen, which will look something like the diagram on page xiii. Its exact display depends on the other applications you have installed on your machine.

2 Click the mouse when the screen arrow is on the Word for Windows window which will have been set up by the installation program.

3 Double click on the Word for Windows icon to load up.

4 The Word for Windows screen will be displayed.

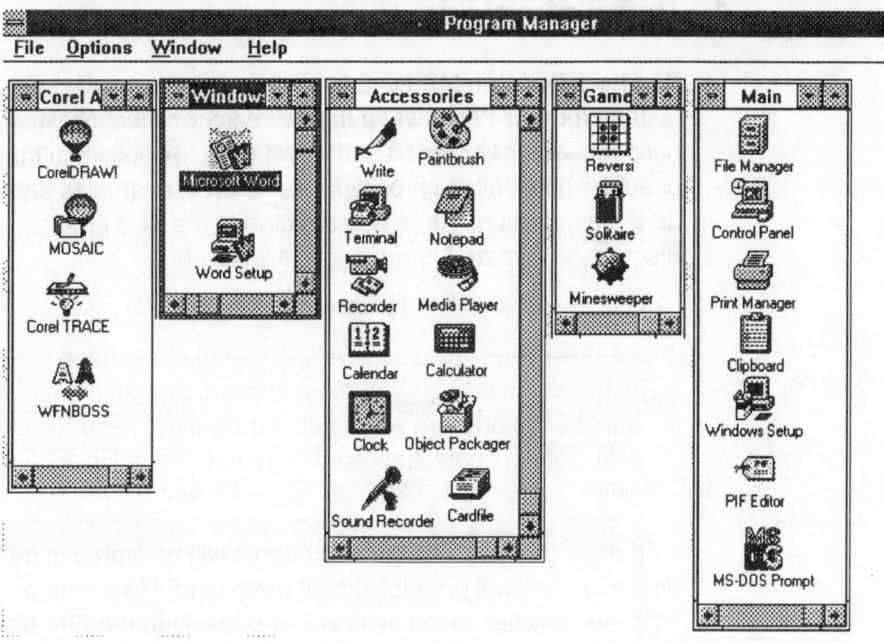

3 Display options

Throughout the units, it is assumed that you have the toolbar, ribbon and ruler displayed and that you are using Page Layout, which allows you to see where the margins are on your page.

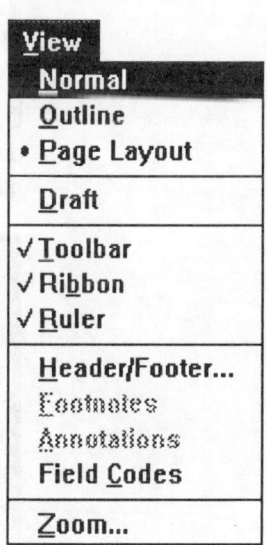

1 Pull down the **View** menu to check whether there are ticks against **Toolbar**, **Ribbon** and **Ruler** and a dot beside **Page Layout**, as shown.

2 If any of the options is not as shown, select it. Repeat this process until all items are correctly selected.

3 You should now have margins showing and the toolbar, ribbon and ruler onscreen.

4 Using directories

Windows uses the MS-DOS file hierarchy, ie a 'tree' structure. When you install Word for Windows, a main directory called **Winword** is created on your hard disk (usually **C** or **D**) at the first level, as shown in the diagram. This directory holds all the programs, templates, examples and clipart which make up the application. Three sub-directories are also created, as shown in the diagram, ie Clipart, Library and Winword.cbt.

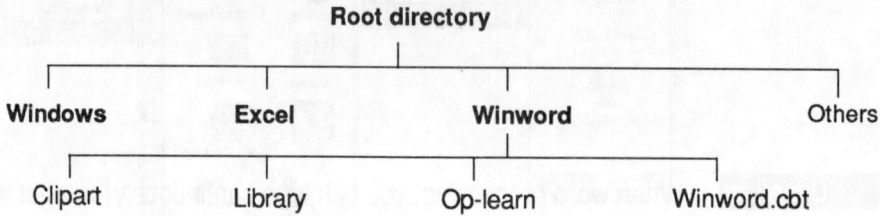

By default (preset), all your documents will be stored in the **Winword** directory. You will probably find it more useful to set up a special directory to hold the activities in the units in this book. Run the **File Manager** from the **Program Manager** window and select **Create Directory** from the **File** menu. Create a sub-directory called **op-learn**.

Opening and saving files

1 When you use the **Open** or **Save** menus, the dialog box will show the available files, as well as the directory structure, as shown below.

2 Double click on the **op-learn** name or icon to open this sub-directory and display its files. This will make this sub-directory the *current* directory, and all files will be saved to it.

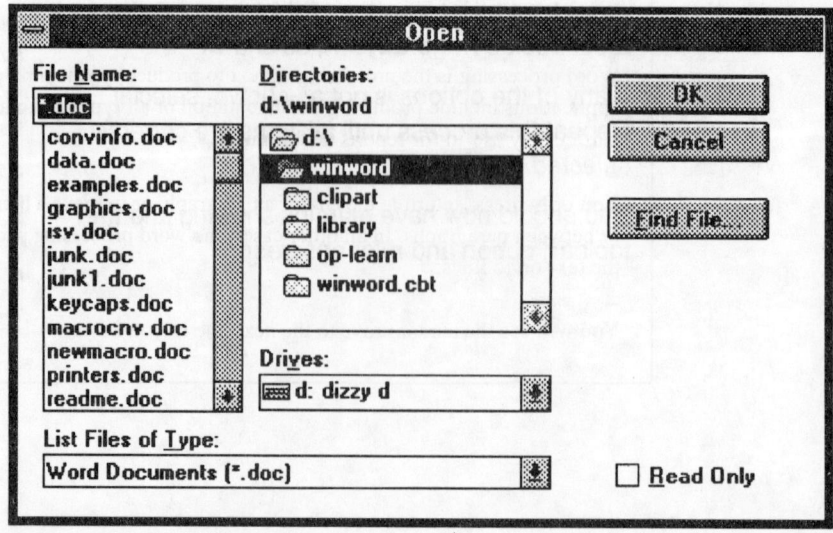

Unit 1

Text entry

When word processing, you can type continuously, without worrying about line endings, margins, tabs, pagination and so on. All these can be set later, if you do not want to use the default settings (those preset for you by Word).

- Keying in text
- Using Backspace delete to correct mistakes as you type
- Saving text to disk
- Printing text

You do not press the **Return** (Enter) key at the end of each line, only at the end of a paragraph or after a heading. (In the sample below ↵ stands for **Return**)

Word Processing↵
↵
Word processing is the processing of text to produce typed work by computer. Its applications include producing documentation of all types and editing text, which is particularly useful for reports and minutes.↵
↵
You only press Return at the end of a paragraph, or to make a blank line after a heading or between paragraphs. In all other cases, the word processing package will organise the text on to lines.↵
↵
You will see the cursor move to the next line as you key.↵

1.1 Typing text in a new file

1 Load up Word for Windows to display a blank screen. The cursor, a flashing vertical bar, is at the top left of the screen, just below the menu bar. This marks the position where the text you type will be displayed.

2 Key in the text, pressing the space bar once at the end of each word and after commas and full stops. The cursor will move as you type.

3 If you type an incorrect character, use the **Backspace** key to move the cursor back over it and delete it.

4 Press the **Return** (Enter) key *only*:

- at the end of paragraphs
- after a heading
- for a blank line after headings/paragraphs.

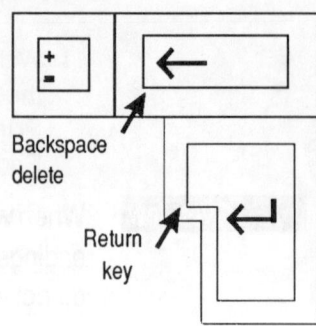

Backspace
delete

Return
key

---

1 Load up Word for Windows

2 Type in the following heading and paragraph, pressing **Return** twice at the end of the heading and once at the end of the paragraph

3 Use the Backspace key to delete any characters you key wrongly

---

WORD PROCESSING

Word processing has steadily increased in popularity since the early 1970s. Operators have been delighted with the ease of keyboarding and the facilities for correction and editing. Repetitive typing has become a thing of the past and all work can be produced to a very high standard.

1.2 Saving new text to disk

1 Select the **Save** button from the toolbar or select **Save** from the **File** menu to display the appropriate dialog box.

2 Key in your selected file name (up to 8 letters or digits), and select **OK**. The **Summary Info** dialog box will be displayed. Click **OK** again.

3 The disk light will flash very quickly as the file is saved and then the file name will be displayed on the title bar at the top of the screen.

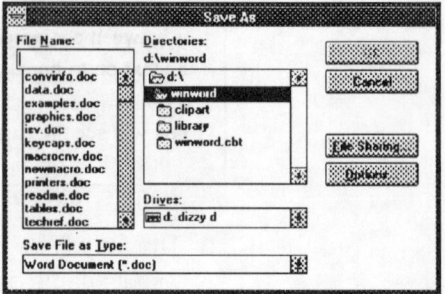

1.3 Printing the text on screen

Important Before you print, you should make the following checks to your printer. It should be:
- switched on
- on-line
- loaded with paper;

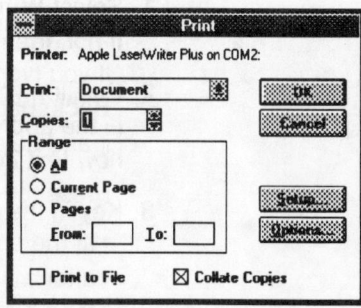

1 With your text displayed on screen, select the **Print** button from the toolbar or select **Print** from the **File** menu to display the Print dialog box.

2 Check your printer and select **OK** to print your text.

Activity 2

1 Save the paragraph of text you have just entered, typing in the name **UNIT1-1**. The text will be saved with the name **UNIT1-1.DOC**; DOC is the file extension added automatically to all standard Word for Windows documents

2 Print the text which is still on screen

1.4 Clearing text and opening a new window

1 Select the **New** button from the toolbar or **New** from the **File** menu. A dialog box will be displayed.

2 Select **OK** to accept the default template **NORMAL**.

3 A new empty window will be displayed, with the name **DOCUMENTx**, where x is the number of windows you have used so far, in this session.

1.5 Retrieving text from disk

1 Select the **Open** button from the toolbar or **Open** from the **File** menu to display the File selection dialog box.

2 Highlight the name of the file you want to retrieve and select **OK**.

3 The file will be displayed on screen, with its name on the title bar.

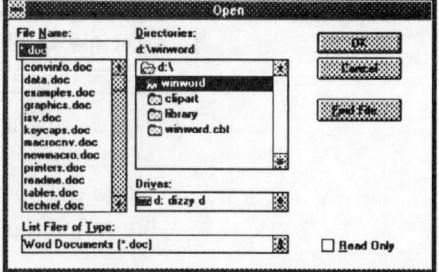

1.6 Adding to existing text

Using Word for Windows, you can have several files available at once. When you save a file and select **New** to begin another one, the first file is still in a window *behind* the current one, and will be listed in the **Window** menu.

1 Select **Window** on the menu bar. If your existing file is listed, then select it. If not, then open it using the **Open** button from the toolbar.

2 Position your text cursor at the end of the text by clicking the mouse button in the appropriate position and, if a blank line is needed to separate the new text from the old, press **Return** to insert one.

3 Key in the additional text, using Backspace to delete any mistakes.

1.7 Saving existing text to disk

1 When you have made any additions or corrections to the text, select the **Save** button from the toolbar.

2 A dialog box may be displayed. If so, select **OK** to confirm the default and save with the same name as before.

Important If the document you are working on already has a name, then **Save** will resave with the same name. To save with a **new** name, select **Save As** from the **File** menu. You will then have the opportunity to key in a new name.

Activity 3
1 Clear the text to display the typing screen
2 Retrieve the file **UNIT1-1.DOC** and add, at the end, the 2 paragraphs shown below
3 Save the text again with the same name

Other useful software is a Thesaurus and there are even programs to pick up grammatical mistakes.

Word processing is very popular with home users and the cost of the machines has dropped so dramatically during recent years that they have become within the reach of many users who had previously been content with a manual, electric or electronic typewriter.

1.8 Closing a file

To remove a file totally from memory, you have to close it. Loading a new file just adds to the list of those available.

1 With the file displayed on screen, select **Close** from the **File** menu.

2 If you have made any changes since you last saved the file, you will be prompted to save it.

3 The file will disappear from screen and a new blank screen will be displayed with the name **DOCUMENTx**.

Activity 4

1 Make sure that you have saved the file **UNIT1-1.DOC** with the extra text you added in Activity 3

2 Close the file and check that its name has disappeared from the list in the **Windows** menu

3 Open the file **UNIT1-1.DOC** and print the complete file, which should look like the example given below

---

WORD PROCESSING

Word processing has steadily increased in popularity since the early 1970s. Operators have been delighted with the ease of keyboarding and the facilities for correction and editing. Repetitive typing has become a thing of the past and all work can be produced to a very high standard.

Other useful software is a Thesaurus and there are even programs to pick up grammatical mistakes.

Word processing is very popular with home users and the cost of the machines has dropped so dramatically during recent years that they have become within the reach of many users who had previously been content with a manual, electric or electronic typewriter.

1.9 Adding summary information

A Word for Windows document has some information associated with it, which is saved with it and can be inserted into the text if needed. The author's name is entered automatically, but can be changed. You can enter the data when you first save the file, or edit it at any time by selecting **Summary Info** from the **File** menu.

FIELD	CONTENTS
Filename	The name of the file
Directory	The directory in which the file is stored on disk
Title	A title, longer and more descriptive than the filename.
Subject	A short description of the file's contents
Author	Name assigned on installation, but can be changed
Keywords	Special topics in the document
Comments	Any additional remarks you want to keep with the text

1   Key in your text and select the **Save** button from the toolbar. Key in the filename as usual and select **OK**.

2   The Summary Info dialog box will be displayed.

3   Enter text in any field.

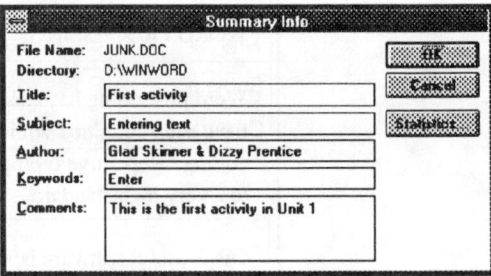

Activity 5

1   Clear the screen if necessary
2   Key in the text given below, pressing **Return** twice at the end of each heading and at the end of each paragraph
3   Save the text with the file name **UNIT1-2.DOC**

WP OPERATORS

When operating a WP for any length of time it is important to ensure that working conditions are comfortable. If a few simple precautions are not observed, the work can lead to headaches and backaches.

THE VDU

The VDU should be sited so that there is no reflection on the screen, which could cause eyestrain.

Activity 6

1 Open the file **UNIT1-2.DOC** or select it from the **Windows** menu, if it is not already on screen
2 Add to the text the additional third heading and paragraph shown below
3 Resave the file with the same name

DESK AND CHAIR

The workstation or desk should be at a comfortable height for the operator and an adjustable chair should be used so that the back is supported at all times whilst the feet are flat on the floor.

Activity 7

1 Open the file **UNIT1-2.DOC** or select it from the **Windows** menu, if it is not already on screen
2 Select **Summary Info** from the **File** menu and enter text in the fields as shown below
3 Save the file and print it, so that you have a paper copy. It should look like the sample shown below, but not necessarily with the same line endings

FIELD	CONTENTS
Title	Second activity
Subject	Rules for word processing operators
Comments	Demonstration of summary information

WP OPERATORS

When operating a WP for any length of time it is important to ensure that working conditions are comfortable. If a few simple precautions are not observed, the work can lead to headaches and backaches.

THE VDU

The VDU should be sited so that there is no reflection on the screen, which could cause eyestrain.

DESK AND CHAIR

The workstation or desk should be at a comfortable height for the operator and an adjustable chair should be used so that the back is supported at all times whilst the feet are flat on the floor.

---

1 Producing letters and reports

2 Saving text for later use

3 Producing several copies of text

Problem solving

- *The message "This is not a valid filename" is displayed when you have typed in your file name to save the text.*

  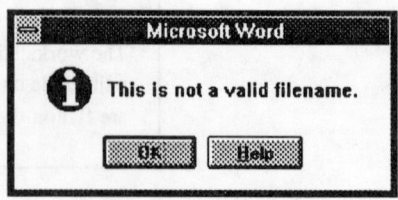

  You used invalid characters in your file name, eg space, / or another special character. You can use only letters, digits and the hyphen (not as the first character). Save again, and use the file name suggested.

- *Your Print command does not work.*

  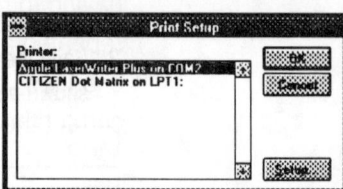

  The printer may have no paper, or be switched off, or not be on-line. If none of these appears to be the problem, then select **Print setup** from the **File** menu to check that the correct printer is highlighted. If not, highlight the correct one and try again.

- *You cannot find your file on the disk.*

  You may not have typed in the name you intended when saving. Look down the list of files displayed. Click on **Read only** to view part of a file, rather than opening and view files with similar names to the one you want. When you find it, click on **Read only** again and open the correct file.

- *Your paragraphs are not in the correct order in one of your documents.*

  The cursor was not at the end of the existing text when you keyed in the extra text. Delete the new text, move the cursor to the end and key the text in again.

- *There is not a blank line between each paragraph.*

  You did not press **Return** to add a blank line before you added text. Position the cursor at the first letter of the paragraph with no blank line before it and press **Return** to insert a blank line.

- *Your Summary Info dialog box disappeared from screen before you had finished entering all the fields.*

  You probably pressed **Return** at the end of an entry, instead of repositioning your cursor, with the mouse, in the next field to be completed. Select **Summary Info** from the **File** menu and complete the fields.

Unit 2

Text editing

Inserting texts and points

Overview   One of the main advantages of word processing is that it saves you from having to rekey text which you have used before; blocks of text can be repeated automatically. You can retrieve your text from disk and make any changes you like. You can even find spelling mistakes and mistypes and correct them automatically.

Existing skills
- Keying in text - Unit 1
- Retrieving text from disk - Unit 1
- Saving and printing text - Unit 1

New skills
- Inserting extra text
- Deleting unwanted text
- Rearranging text
- Copying blocks of text
- Checking spelling

Important   Should you change your mind immediately after you have deleted text, you may reverse the process using the **Undo** button on the toolbar.

Rearranging and copying text are carried out using the Windows Clipboard. Text which is cut or copied is stored in the clipboard and can then be pasted in at the cursor position. All three operations have dedicated buttons on the ribbon.

Cut   Copy   Paste   Undo

2.1 Inserting text

When you use Word for Windows, the setting *Insert* mode is **on** by default. This means that as new characters are keyed, existing text moves to accommodate them.

1 Position your cursor at the point in the existing text where the additional character is to be inserted.

2 Key in the characters which are to be inserted.

Important You can insert Spaces and Returns, as well as ordinary characters like A and D. This will often be necessary to make blank lines and to separate words.

Activity 1

1 If you have already completed Unit 1 and so have **UNIT1-1.DOC** saved to disk, retrieve it and display it on screen
or
If this file is not on disk, key in the heading and first three paragraphs given below, beginning each line at the left hand margin and leaving one clear line after the heading and each paragraph
2 Insert the additional paragraph shown at the end, in the position indicated by the arrow
3 Save with the same name as before

WORD PROCESSING

Word processing has steadily increased in popularity since the early 1970s. Operators have been delighted with the ease of keyboarding and the facilities for correction and editing. Repetitive typing has become a thing of the past and all work can be produced to a very high standard.

→ Other useful software is a Thesaurus and there are even programs to pick up grammatical mistakes.

Word processing is very popular with home users and the cost of the machines has dropped so dramatically during recent years that they have become within the reach of many users who had previously been content with a manual, electric or electronic typewriter.

Even if you are not familiar with the keyboard, you can still use a word processor to good advantage because of the ease of correction. Many operators use a spelling check program to aid in proofreading their work. Although a checker will not pick up such mistakes as 'know' for 'now', it will identify many mistypes.

2.2 Deleting a character

If you have completed Unit 1, you may have already used Backspace delete, which moves the cursor to the left, deleting as it goes. The **Delete** key, shown in the diagram, deletes the character at the cursor position, rather than one to the left.

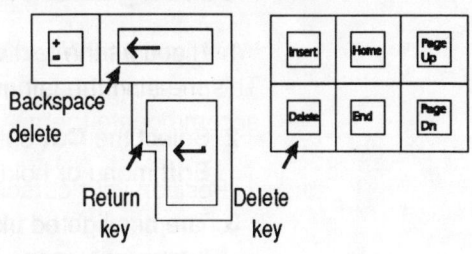

1 Move the cursor to the character to be deleted.

2 Press the Delete key once.

3 Repeat this process, to delete more text.

Important You can delete Spaces and Returns, as well as ordinary characters like A and D. This will often be necessary to remove blank lines and any extra spaces.

Activity 2
1 Retrieve the file **UNIT1-1.DOC**, if it is not already on screen
2 Delete the third paragraph, as marked below
3 Save the new version with the same name and print a copy

WORD PROCESSING

Word processing has steadily increased in popularity since the early 1970s. Operators have been delighted with the ease of keyboarding and the facilities for correction and editing. Repetitive typing has become a thing of the past and all work can be produced to a very high standard.

Even if you are not familiar with the keyboard, you can still use a word processor to good advantage because of the ease of correction. Many operators use a spelling check program to aid in proofreading their work. Although a checker will not pick up such mistakes as 'know' for 'now', it will identify many mistypes.

Other useful software is a Thesaurus and there are even programs to pick up grammatical mistakes.

Word processing is very popular with home users and the cost of the machines has dropped so dramatically during recent years that they have become within the reach of many users who had previously been content with a manual, electric or electronic typewriter.

2.3 Cutting and pasting text

1 Highlight the text with your mouse, by pointing at the first character, pressing the left mouse button and dragging to the end of the text.

2 Select the **Cut** button from the toolbar or alternatively, select **Cut** from the **Edit** menu or hold down the **Shift** key and press the **Delete** key.

3 The highlighted block will disappear from screen. It has been saved temporarily in the Windows clipboard.

4 Position your cursor at the new position for the block and select the **Paste** button from the toolbar, or alternatively select **Paste** from the **Edit** menu or hold down the **Shift** key and press **Insert**.

5 The saved block will be inserted into your text at the cursor.

Activity 3

1 If you have already completed Unit 1 and so have **UNIT1-2.DOC** saved to disk, retrieve it and display it on screen
or
If this file is not on disk, key in the headings and paragraphs given below, beginning each line at the left hand margin and leaving one clear line after each heading and paragraph

2 Move the last heading and paragraph as indicated below, deleting and inserting **Returns**, as required, to give the correct display

3 Save the new version and print, if required

WP OPERATORS

When operating a WP for any length of time it is important to ensure that working conditions are comfortable. If a few simple precautions are not observed, the work can lead to headaches and backaches.

 THE VDU

The VDU should be sited so that there is no reflection on the screen, which could cause eyestrain.

DESK AND CHAIR

The workstation or desk should be at a comfortable height for the operator and an adjustable chair should be used so that the back is supported at all times whilst the feet are flat on the floor.

2.4 Deleting blocks of text

There is a method by which you can delete a whole piece of text at once, rather than by repeatedly using the Backspace or Delete keys, which is slow and can be inaccurate.

1 Highlight the text as before.

2 Select the **Cut** button from the toolbar or press the **Delete** key.

2.5 Undeleting text

1 Immediately you have deleted a character or a marked block of text, select the **Undo** button from the toolbar.

2 The deleted text will be replaced in the same position.

Important **Undo** works only immediately after a deletion, and then only for one character if you have deleted with the **Backspace** or **Delete** keys.

Activity 4

1 Retrieve the file **UNIT1-2.DOC**, if it is not already on screen
2 Delete the second paragraph, by highlighting
3 Use Undo to replace the text

WP OPERATORS

When operating a WP for any length of time it is important to ensure that working conditions are comfortable. If a few simple precautions are not observed, the work can lead to headaches and backaches.

DESK AND CHAIR

The workstation or desk should be at a comfortable height for the operator and an adjustable chair should be used so that the back is supported at all times whilst the feet are flat on the floor.

THE VDU

The VDU should be sited so that there is no reflection on the screen, which could cause eyestrain.

---

1 Open the file **UNIT1-1.DOC**
2 Cut the last paragraph and paste it in, as shown
3 Save and print, if required

WORD PROCESSING

Word processing has steadily increased in popularity since the early 1970s. Operators have been delighted with the ease of keyboarding and the facilities for correction and editing. Repetitive typing has become a thing of the past and all work can be produced to a very high standard.

Even if you are not familiar with the keyboard, you can still use a word processor to good advantage because of the ease of correction. Many operators use a spelling check program to aid in proof reading their work. Although a checker will not pick up such mistakes as 'know' for 'now', it will identify many mistypes.

Word processing is very popular with home users and the cost of the machines has dropped so dramatically during recent years that they have become within the reach of many users who had previously been content with a manual, electric or electronic typewriter.

2.6 Copying blocks of text

You can save a considerable amount of keying time by copying blocks of text which are needed in several places.

1 Highlight the text block, as before.

2 Select the **Copy** button from the toolbar or, alternatively, select **Copy** from the **Edit** menu, or hold down **Ctrl** and press **Insert**. A copy of the text will be saved in the Windows (version 3) clipboard.

3 Position the cursor where the second copy is to appear in the text.

4 Select the **Paste** button from the toolbar or, alternatively, select **Paste** from the **Edit** menu, or hold down **Shift** and press **Insert**. The text will be pasted in at the cursor.

2.7 Checking spelling

1 Position the cursor at the beginning of the text. Select the **Spelling** button from the toolbar or select **Spelling** from the **Tools** menu to display the dialog box.

2 Each word not found in the dictionary will be displayed in turn. You can make any of the choices shown for each word.

```
┌─────────────────────────────────────────────────────┐
│▓▓▓            Spelling: English (UK)                 │
│ Not in Dictionary:  curser                           │
│                                                      │
│ Change To:    cursor          [ Ignore ] [Ignore All]│
│ Suggestions:  cursor                                 │
│               curler          [ Change ] [Change All]│
│               curse                                  │
│               curare          [  Add  ]              │
│               cures                                  │
│               cursed          [         ] [ Cancel ] │
│                                                      │
│ Add Words To: CUSTOM.DIC      [ Options ]            │
└─────────────────────────────────────────────────────┘
```

3 For any word which is not a real misspelling, perhaps a name which will not be in the dictionary, you can **Ignore**. You can **Add** any special words for your area of interest to a personal dictionary.

4 Select the correct word from the suggestions listed on screen for real mistypes or misspellings and click **Change**. If you have so mistyped the word that it bears no resemblance to the word intended, there may be no suggestions which are correct; you can correct the word manually, using insertion and deletion.

Activity 5

1 Clear the screen, if necessary
2 Key in the following notice for display in newsagents' windows
3 Use the spell checker to correct the common spelling mistakes made in it
4 Mark and copy the whole notice, so that it fits 3 times on a sheet of A4 paper, leaving several blank lines between copies, for cutting
5 Save as file **UNIT2-1.DOC** and print a copy

ACCOMODATION WANTED

Mature student, clean, non-smoker, requires furnished room with shared facilitys from September, in Bridgford area.

Serius replies only, please, to Alex on 818818 (daytime only before 5 pm).

Good refferences supplied.

ACCOMODATION WANTED

Mature student, clean, non-smoker, requires furnished room with shared facilitys from September, in Bridgford area.

Serius replies only, please, to Alex on 818818 (daytime only before 5 pm).

---

1 Redrafting reports and minutes

2 Using similar pieces of text to produce new ones

3 Checking spelling in initial proofreading

Problem solving • *When you try to insert text, the existing text is deleted and replaced by the new text you are keying in.*

You have probably pressed the **Insert** key by mistake, which switches word processing into *Overtype* mode, ie keying in replaces text, rather than inserting as usual. If you have, the letters **OVR** will be displayed at the bottom right hand side of the screen. Press the **Insert** key again, to reverse this and rekey the letters you have deleted.

• *The text you retrieved is not what you wanted.*

Either you highlighted the wrong file name, or you saved the file with the wrong name. **Close** the file on screen, select **Find File** from the **File** menu again and look through all the files to find the one you want. Highlight it and click **OK** to open it.

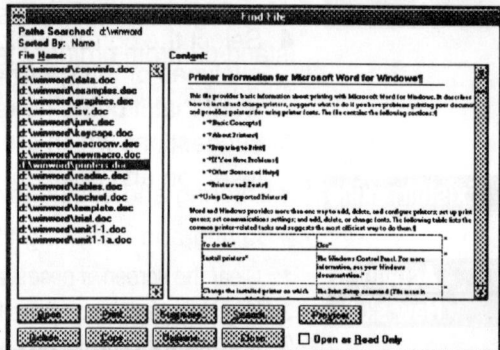

• *You cannot remember the name of the file you want.*

Select **Find File** from the **File** menu to display the names of all files. Highlight a name to look at the text in the window displayed.

• *There is no blank line between two paragraphs, but more than one blank line between others.*

You did not include the blank line in your block when you highlighted. Position the cursor on the first letter of the paragraph with no blank line before it and press **Return** to insert a blank line. Then position the cursor on the first line of the paragraph with more than one blank line and press Backspace delete to get rid of a blank line. Repeat, if necessary.

• *Your paragraphs are in a different order from the sample given.*

Your cursor was in the wrong position when you moved or copied a block of text. Select the block again and move it again, making sure to position the cursor correctly before completing the move or copy.

• *You have chosen the wrong word to replace a spelling mistake.*

Position the cursor at the beginning of the word, use the Delete key to delete it and key in the correct word.

Unit 3

Headings

Overview

Headings can be emphasised in a number of different ways, to make them stand out from ordinary text. The most commonly used methods are to centre, underline or embolden the text.

Existing skills

- Entering and editing text - Units 1 and 2
- Saving and retrieving files - Units 1 and 2

New skills

- Centring text on a line
- Enhancing text - using special features for emphasis eg emboldening, underlining, italics

Important

Emboldening, underlining, italics and centring are all examples of operations best carried out using buttons on the toolbar, rather than menu options, as this is much faster.

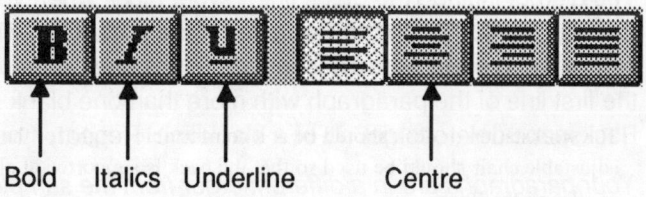

Bold   Italics   Underline   Centre

3.1 Centring text for headings

Headings can be centred to create an attractive display. Centring is shown on screen, exactly as it will be printed.

1 Key in the text, starting each line at the left margin.

2 Position the cursor anywhere in the paragraph to be centred at any time, ie either before, after or during keying in, and select the **Centre** button from the toolbar.

3 Follow the same procedure for each paragraph or line to be centred.

Important If you are centring text as you key in, then you must select the **Left Align** button from the toolbar when you key in any line or paragraph which is not to be centred. Then select the **Centre** button for the next line or paragraph to be centred.

Activity 1

1 If you have already completed Units 1 and 2 and so have **UNIT1-2.DOC** saved to disk, open it and display it on screen
or
If the file is not on disk, key in the text given below, beginning each line at the left margin and leaving one clear line after each heading and paragraph
2 Centre each heading line
3 Save the text with filename **UNIT3-1.DOC** and print one copy

---

WP OPERATORS

When operating a WP for any length of time it is important to ensure that working conditions are comfortable. If a few simple precautions are not observed, the work can lead to headaches and backaches.

DESK AND CHAIR

The workstation or desk should be at a comfortable height for the operator and an adjustable chair should be used so that the back is supported at all times whilst the feet are flat on the floor.

THE VDU

The VDU should be sited so that there is no reflection on the screen, which could cause eyestrain.

---

1 Open the file **UNIT3-1.DOC**, if it is not already on screen
2 Key in the additional heading, centring it before entry
3 Add the extra paragraph, as shown
4 Proofread the text on screen and make any changes necessary
5 Save the file again and print a revised copy

WP OPERATORS

When operating a WP for any length of time it is important to ensure that working conditions are comfortable. If a few simple precautions are not observed, the work can lead to headaches and backaches.

DESK AND CHAIR

The workstation or desk should be at a comfortable height for the operator and an adjustable chair should be used so that the back is supported at all times whilst the feet are flat on the floor.

THE VDU

The VDU should be sited so that there is no reflection on the screen, which could cause eyestrain.

BREAKS

Breaks are important and an operator would be well advised not to work more than 2 hours at a VDU without a break.

3.2 Enhancing existing text

Enhancing *existing* text is achieved by highlighting the text to be enhanced and then applying the enhancement. Underlining, emboldening, italics and other special effects are available.

1 Select the text to be enhanced with the mouse.

2 Select the **Bold**, **Underline** or **Italics** button from the toolbar.

3 The text is now shown on the screen with your chosen enhancement.

1 Retrieve the text stored as **UNIT3-1.DOC**
2 Underline the headings as shown, using the **Underline** button
3 Save and print one copy

WP OPERATORS

When operating a WP for any length of time it is important to ensure that working conditions are comfortable. If a few simple precautions are not observed, the work can lead to headaches and backaches.

DESK AND CHAIR

The workstation or desk should be at a comfortable height for the operator and an adjustable chair should be used so that the back is supported at all times whilst the feet are flat on the floor.

THE VDU

The VDU should be sited so that there is no reflection on the screen, which could cause eyestrain.

BREAKS

Breaks are important and an operator would be well advised not to work more than 2 hours at a VDU without a break.

3.3 Enhancing text as you key in

1 At the beginning of the text to be enhanced, select the appropriate button from the toolbar. You will notice that the button is displayed *pushed in*.
2 Continue keying in to the end of the enhanced text, then select the button again, to stop the effect. The button will be displayed normally again.

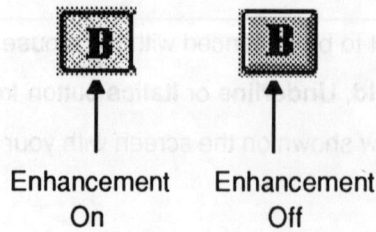

Enhancement   Enhancement
On   Off

Activity 4

1 Key in the text given below, using underlining, bold text and italics as shown
2 Centre each line as shown and save as **UNIT3-2.DOC**
3 Proofread on screen and make any necessary changes
4 Print one copy

SAMSON COLLEGE OF ADULT EDUCATION

<u>PHOTOGRAPHIC EXHIBITION</u>

10 March 9 am - 5 pm

<u>Admission Free</u>

Activity 5

1 Key in the text given below, using underlining and bold text as shown
2 Centre the headings as shown
3 Check the display and make any necessary corrections
4 Save the text as **UNIT3-3.DOC** and print one copy

WESTERHAM HOTEL

ANTIQUES VALUATION EVENING

7 July 7.30 pm - 10 pm

<u>Featuring Arthur Nolty (from Southalls)</u>

Bring your treasures for valuation

<u>Tickets £10 including a glass of wine and buffet</u>

All enquiries to Kate Fairmont   (0509 884521)
Westerham Hotel, Courts, Leics,   LE1 5PQ

Further uses
1 Emphasising the subject in a letter
2 Emphasising the subject of a memo or report
3 Emphasising side headings
4 Highlighting important issues in a document

Problem solving
- *One or more of the characters, probably the last one, is not enhanced as you intended.*

  You did not select all the characters before highlighting. Perhaps your cursor was *on* the last character, rather than *after* it? Select the character(s) a second time and apply the enhancement again.

- *Text following the piece you intended to underline is also underlined.*

  You did not select the underlining button again at the end of the text to switch off the enhancement, so the button is still *pushed*. Select the text which should not be underlined and select the button again to remove the enhancement.

- *Text following the piece you intended to embolden is also bold.*

  You did not select the bold button again at the end of the text to switch off the enhancement. Select the text which should not be bold and select the button again to remove the enhancement.

- *All your text is centred, not just the headings.*

  You did not turn off centring when you wanted to go back to left alignment, when keying in text. Position your cursor in each line or paragraph which is not intended to be centred and select the **Left Align** button from the toolbar.

Unit 4

Notices and programmes

Overview

Notices and programmes can be made attractive using simple display features such as vertical and horizontal centring, underlining, emboldening, changes in text size, italics and right alignment.

Existing skills

- Entering and editing text, saving and retrieving files - Units 1 and 2
- Centring a single line of text - Unit 3
- Enhancing text and using blocks - Units 2 and 3

New skills

- Centring a block of text
- Centring text vertically on a page
- Aligning text to the right margin
- Changing text size

Important

You will need to work out vertical centring yourself. The text will, however, only be printed vertically centred if the paper in the printer is set correctly.

MENU

Fresh Asparagus
Country Pate

Chicken Marengo
Vegetarian Lasagne

Strawberries and cream
Raspberry Bombe

Cheese and biscuits

Coffee with mints

4.1 Vertical centring

1 Count the number of lines of text you have, including blank lines.

2 Subtract this number from the total for the page. This will vary according to the defaults set on your machine.

3 Divide the answer by 2 and insert this number of lines before the text.

Activity 1

1 If you have already completed Unit 3, so **UNIT3-3.DOC** is saved to disk, open it and display it on screen
   or
   If the file is not on disk, key in the text given below, using the display shown

2 Centre lines of text, as shown and centre the text vertically

3 Save the text with filename **UNIT4-1.DOC**

WESTERHAM HOTEL

ANTIQUES VALUATION EVENING

7 July 7.30 pm - 10 pm

<u>**Featuring Arthur Nolty (from Southalls)**</u>

Bring your treasures for valuation

<u>Tickets £10 including a glass of wine and buffet</u>

All enquiries to Kate Fairmont (0509 884521)
Westerham Hotel, Courts, Leics, LE1 5PQ

Activity 2

1 If you have completed Unit 3 and so **UNIT3-2.DOC** is saved to disk, open it
   or
   If the file is not on disk, key in the text given below, following the display as shown

2 Centre the text vertically

3 Save the text with filename **UNIT4-2.DOC**

SAMSON COLLEGE OF ADULT EDUCATION

<u>PHOTOGRAPHIC EXHIBITION</u>

10 March 9 am - 5 pm

<u>**Admission Free**</u>

4.2 Previewing text

Previewing allows you to check the display of the whole page before printing.

1 Display your text on screen, retrieving it from disk if necessary.

2 Select **Print Preview** from the **File** menu to see your text on screen.

3 Select **Cancel** to return to your text.

1 Open the file **UNIT4-2.DOC**, if it is not already on screen
2 Preview the text to check the display
3 Make any necessary changes to the display and print out a copy

4.3 Centring an existing block of text

It is not necessary to centre each line of text individually. Instead you can centre a number of lines at once, or even a complete page of text.

1 Move the cursor into the margin beside the first line of those to be centred and select all the lines to be centred.

2 Select the **Centre** button from the toolbar.

1 Retrieve the text stored as **UNIT4-1.DOC**
2 Centre the whole notice as shown
3 Save, preview and print one copy

WESTERHAM HOTEL

ANTIQUES VALUATION EVENING

7 July 7.30 pm - 10 pm

Featuring Arthur Nolty (from Southalls)

Bring your treasures for valuation

Tickets £10 including a glass of wine and buffet

All enquiries to Kate Fairmont   (0509 884521)
Westerham Hotel, Courts, Leics, LE1 5PQ

4.4 Centring all text while keying in

1 Clear the screen to key in a new file.

2 Before entering any text, select the **Centre** button from the toolbar.

3 Key in the text as normal. It will be centred automatically, as this format has been selected.

4 When ordinary left justified text is required again, select the **Centre** button again and continue keying in.

Activity 5

1 Key in the text below, using the **Centre** button to begin and end centring
2 Apply underline and bold as shown
3 Preview and make any necessary changes
4 Save as file **UNIT4-3.DOC** and print one copy

SAMSON COLLEGE OF ADULT EDUCATION

A MUSICAL EVENING WITH KENNETH HAYNES

30 April at 8 pm

Spring is here
Lilacs
Chrysanthemums
In Nature's Realm
Flower Song

4.5 Aligning new text to the right margin

You can right align existing text or you can align as you key in.

1 With the cursor immediately before the text to be right aligned, select the **Right Align** button from the toolbar.

2 Key in the text to be aligned, if necessary.

4.6 Aligning existing text

Select the text in the usual way and then select the **Right Align** button.

4.7 Changing text size

Type size in points	Ascenders, x-height, Descenders

The text sizes you can use depend on the printer you are using. Word for Windows provides a large number of possible sizes, measured in point sizes, from which you may choose. There are 72 points to 1 inch.

1 Mark the word or block of text which is to have its size changed, using the mouse (*see* Unit 2), or by selecting before keying in.

2 Select the downward arrow button beside the TEXT SIZE from the ribbon and then the size you want from the list displayed.

Important   If you choose text larger than about 14 point for a heading using this method, you will need 2 blank lines after it, otherwise the text will look very cramped.

Activity 8
1 Clear the screen, if necessary
2 Key in the text for the ticket shown below, leaving 2 blank lines after each of the large headings
3 Use right alignment and centring to produce the display given
4 Preview to check the display and text sizes
5 Make any changes necessary, save as **UNIT4-4.DOC** and print a copy

---

ST PETER'S SOCIAL CLUB

Present:

Old Tyme Music Hall

8 pm Saturday 2 March

at the Church Hall

Tickets £2.50

Senior Citizens **£2**
Children under 12 **£1.25**

---

1 Producing tickets for fetes, concerts, parties

2 Producing invitations for parties, weddings and other celebrations

3 Making simple handbills and advertisements

4 Once you have learned how to produce labels (*see* Unit 16), you will be able to use these facilities to make smaller tickets and labels, fitting as many as 6 on an A4 sheet for printing

Problem solving

• *One or more of the characters you enlarged, probably the last one, is not the same size as the others.*

You did not select all the characters before enlarging. Perhaps your cursor or mouse pointer was on the last character, rather than after it? Select the character(s) a second time and choose the size again.

• *Your lines of enlarged text are very cramped when printed, perhaps even overlapping.*

You did not leave 2 blank lines between them. Position the cursor in the blank line between the lines of text and press **Return** to insert an additional line.

• *You cannot get back to your text after you have selected a point size.*

You need to position your cursor in the text with the mouse.

• *You have keyed in text to the point size box.*

You need to position your cursor in the text again, using the mouse, as soon as you have selected the point size.

• *Your heading text is smaller than the ordinary text, instead of larger.*

You have chosen a smaller text size rather than a larger one. This is probably because you are more used to measuring text size in characters per inch, where the larger the number, the smaller the text. Remember that font sizes are measured in points, fractions of an inch, so the larger the number, the larger the text.

• *You have selected the **Help** menu and it still displayed on screen, although you have finished with it.*

Click the mouse outside the **Help** window, ie in the Word window. This will make the document the current window and the **Help** screen will disappear from the screen.

Unit 5

Indented paragraphs

Overview A paragraph may be indented from both margins to give emphasis. To give a neat appearance to numbered paragraphs, the text can be indented to the first tab position, leaving the numbers clearly displayed at the left margin.

Existing skills
- Deleting text - Unit 2
- Inserting text - Unit 2
- Retrieving a file from disk - Unit 2

New skills
- Setting a temporary left margin
- Numbering and indenting paragraphs

Important When numbered points are used, the most attractive display is to indent the paragraph after the number, giving a temporary left margin.

This paragraph is not indented at all, but goes right across the page from one margin to the other.↵
↵
1   This is a numbered, indented paragraph, where the text is set to a temporary left margin, until you press Return at the end of the paragraph.↵
↵
This is a fully indented paragraph, where the whole paragraph is inset from the left margin. This feature also lasts until the Return key is pressed at the end of the paragraph.↵

Unindent ⟶  ⟵ **Indent**

5.1 Numbering and indenting text

1 Position the cursor in the first paragraph to be numbered and select the **Numbering** button from the toolbar. The number **1** will be inserted and the remainder of the paragraph indented to the first tab stop.

2 Follow this process for each other paragraph in turn.

Activity 1

1 Clear the screen, if necessary
2 Key in the text shown below, numbering as you go
3 Proofread and make any amendments, save as **UNIT5-1.DOC** and print one copy

---

Advantages of Word Processing

1 Reduces repetitive typing. Standard documents can be reproduced automatically and individual details added.

2 Enables redrafts to be made easily. Insertions, deletions and block moves all save retyping.

3 Facilitates the production of immaculate work.

Activity 2

1 If you have already completed Unit 3 and so have **UNIT3-1.DOC** saved to disk, open it and delete all headings except the first one and the extra blank lines
or
If this file is not on disk, key in the text shown with a clear line between each paragraph
2 Save the text as **UNIT3-1.DOC**

WP OPERATORS

When operating a WP for any length of time it is important to ensure that working conditions are comfortable. If a few simple precautions are not observed, the work can lead to headaches and backaches.

The workstation or desk should be at a comfortable height for the operator and an adjustable chair should be used so that the back is supported at all times whilst the feet are flat on the floor.

The VDU should be sited so that there is no reflection on the screen, which could cause eyestrain.

Breaks are important and an operator would be well advised not to work more than 2 hours at a VDU without a break.

Activity 3

1 Open the file **UNIT3-1.DOC**, if it is not already on screen
2 Number the paragraphs as shown
3 Check the display and the spelling, save and print one copy

---

WP OPERATORS

1 When operating a WP for any length of time it is important to ensure that working conditions are comfortable. If a few simple precautions are not observed, the work can lead to headaches and backaches.

2 The workstation or desk should be at a comfortable height for the operator and an adjustable chair should be used so that the back is supported at all times whilst the feet are flat on the floor.

3 The VDU should be sited so that there is no reflection on the screen, which could cause eyestrain.

4 Breaks are important and an operator would be well advised not to work more than 2 hours at a VDU without a break.

5.2 Indenting paragraphs

With the cursor anywhere in the paragraph to be indented, select the **Indent** button from the toolbar. The **Unindent** button reverses the effect.

Activity 4

1 If you have completed Unit 2 and have the amended version of **UNIT1-1.DOC** on disk, open it
   or
   Key in the text below beginning each paragraph at the left margin
2 Inset the second paragraph, as shown. Save and print

Word processing has steadily increased in popularity since the early 1970s. Operators have been delighted with the ease of keyboarding and the facilities for correction and editing. Repetitive typing has become a thing of the past.

    Even if you are not familiar with the keyboard, you can still use a word processor to good advantage because of the ease of correction. Many operators use a spelling check program to aid in proof reading their work. Although a checker will not pick up such mistakes as 'know' for 'now', it will identify many mistypes.

Word processing is very popular with home users and the cost of the machines has dropped so dramatically during recent years that they have become within the reach of many users who had previously been content with a manual, electric or electronic typewriter.

---

1 Indented paragraphs save leaving an extra line space between paragraphs when working in double line spacing

2 Inset paragraphs can be used to highlight prices or other important items in a letter

• *All your text is numbered, rather than just the paragraphs you chose.*

You selected all the paragraphs when you numbered. Highlight each paragraph in turn which does not need numbering and select **Bullets and Numbering** from the **Tools** menu to display the **Bullets and Numbering** dialog box. Click on **Numbered List** and select **Remove**.

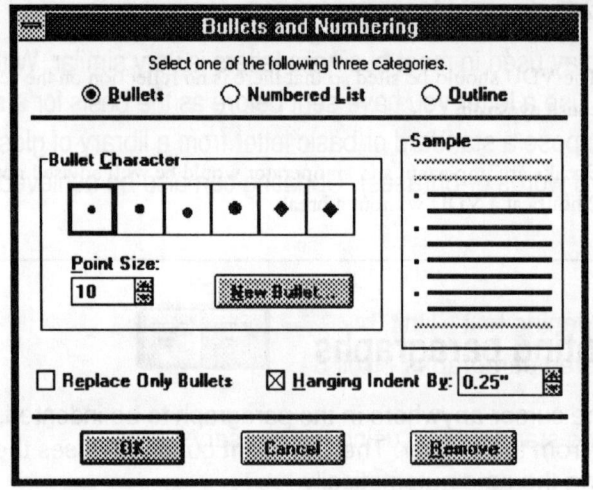

Unit 6

Business letters

The display used in most business letters is very similar. With word processing, you can use a letter you have sent before as the basis for a new one. You can also compose a standard or basic letter from a library of glossary items (standard words or phrases). Updating can also be achieved with search and replace.

Existing skills

- Emboldening text - Unit 3
- Numbered paragraphs - Unit 5

New skills

- Inserting standard text using the glossary
- Inserting the date automatically
- Replacing words and phrases automatically
- Replacing words and phrases selectively

Important

The sample given on the right is the standard layout used in most business letters. It may vary a little, according to a house style in a particular organisation, but this display will always be acceptable. In any case, all the items listed will be needed.

Heading with firm's name

Our Ref:

Today's date

Name
Address

Dear ????

Subject heading

Substance of letter

Yours sincerely

Name of person signing letter
Title of job

6.1 Entering a letter

1 Key in your text using blocked display, ie all lines begin at the left margin, with no indentation, and open puncuation, ie punctuation only in the sentences in the main body of the letter.

2 Position the cursor at the point in the letter where the date is to be inserted.

3 Select **Date and Time** from the **Insert** menu and highlight the date format you want. The date will be inserted at the cursor.

4 Proofread and preview, before saving and printing.

Activity 1

1 Key in the letter shown below, starting all lines at the left margin
2 Embolden the subject heading
3 Spell check to check your text for typing mistakes, then make any necessary corrections
4 Save as **UNIT6-1.DOC** and print

Today's date

Mr M Shah
311 Gelford Road
LEICESTER
LE10 5GR

Dear Mr Shah

Wednesday Club Supper, 5 May

With reference to our telephone conversation of yesterday, I write to confirm that I would be happy to prepare a cold buffet for your group at a cost of £3 per head.

However, as I explained to you on the telephone, should you want a hot meal, the cheapest I could provide would be £3.95 for either plaice or egg and chips, served with a selection of vegetables and a salad garnish.

I look forward to receiving your confirmation of final numbers and menu choice in the near future. If I can be of any further assistance, please do give me a ring.

Yours sincerely

Kerry Asher

Enc

6.2 Setting up a phrase as a glossary item

1 Frequently used phrases can be typed, stored in the Glossary and recalled each time they are needed. Type the phrase, exactly as you want it to be stored, for example, with 2 **Returns** to give an accompanying blank line.

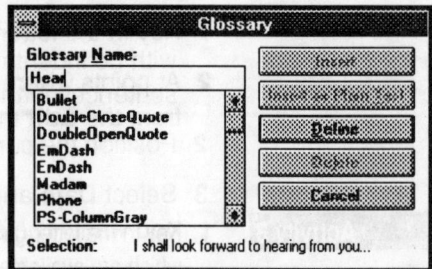

2 Highlight the text and select **Glossary** from the **Edit** menu to display the **Glossary** dialog box.

3 Key in a short name for your glossary item and select **Define** to confirm the name and the text to be used.

4 Set up the other glossary items in the same way.

6.3 Using a glossary item to insert a phrase

1 Position the cursor in the text where the phrase is to be inserted.

2 Select the text **Glossary** from the **Edit** menu. Use the scroll bar to display the name of the item you want, select it and then **Insert**. The stored phrase will be inserted in your text.

Activity 2

1 Clear the screen, if necessary

2 Set up the 10 phrases given in the table below as glossary items, using the names suggested. The symbol ↵ after the text means press Return for an additional blank line

3 Try out the items to make sure they work, proofread and spell check

4 Replace any items which need corrections by setting them up again with the same name and selecting **Define** again

PHRASE	SUGGESTED NAME
Dear Sir ↵	SIR
Dear Madam ↵	MADAM
Thank you for your letter.	THANK
With reference to our telephone conversation	PHONE
I shall look forward to hearing from you. ↵	HEAR
With best wishes ↵	WISHES
Yours sincerely ↵ ↵ ↵ ↵	YRSINC
Douglas Osiejuk ↵	DO
Enc	E

6.4 Using glossary items in a letter

1 Key in the letter as normal, starting all lines at the left margin.

2 At points where an appropriate glossary has been stored, select **Glossary** from the **Edit** menu to insert the stored phrase.

Activity 3

1 Key in the letter given below, using the glossary items to insert stored phrases. The ones which are available are marked with a box

2 Check that you have the correct spacing, insert any additional blank lines which you require, save as **UNIT6-2.DOC** and print

Today's date

Clerk to Northwood Parish Council
29 Windmill Lane
Northwood
North Devon
EX39 2JB

Dear Sir

Maintenance of Northwood Playing Field

With reference to our telephone conversation of today, I have pleasure in submitting the following quotation for the maintenance of Northwood Playing Field:

21 cuts to Cricket Square and Cricket Pitch.

9 mows/trims of field surrounds, including play area, surrounding pavilion and in front of tennis courts and around the saplings alongside the field.

All areas to be maintained using own equipment and fuel.

Price £1100

I shall look forward to hearing from you.

Yours sincerely

Douglas Osiejuk

6.5 Selective search and replace

1 Select **Replace** from the **Edit** menu to display the **Replace** dialog box.

2 Key the characters to be re-placed in the **Find What** box.

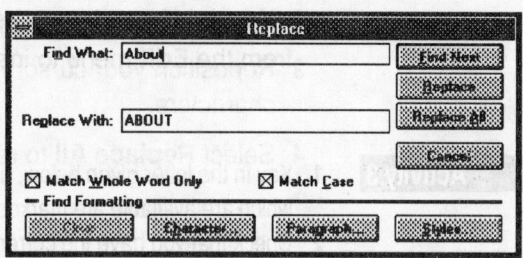

3 Reposition the cursor in the **Replace With** box and key the replacement characters.

4 Click **Find Next**. Then select **Replace** or **Find Next** to replace or move on.

Activity 4

1 Key in the letter given below, using standard letter layout and inserting the current date automatically

2 Use selective replacement to change the colour of the clothes from Black to Grey

3 Save as **UNIT6-3.DOC** and print one copy

Today's date

Ms A Black
Manageress
E & G Modes
Avebury Way
MILTON KEYNES   MK14 0RD

Dear Ms Black

Thank you for your telephone enquiry today regarding our summer range of 'Ginelli'. I have in stock the following fashions which I think will fulfil your requirements:

5 Rose pink suits, sizes 12-14 @ £200 each
10 Black and white two pieces, sizes 10-16 @ £150 each
20 Black spot skirts, sizes 10-16 @ £70 each
20 Black spot blouses, sizes 10-16 @ £59 each
8 Black summer jackets @ £79 each

I look forward to hearing from you.

Yours sincerely

Nicholos Selepegno
Managing Director

6.6 Automatic search and replace

1 Select **Replace** from the **Edit** menu to display the **Replace** dialog box.

2 Key the characters to be replaced in the **Find What** box.

3 Reposition your cursor in the **Replace With** box and key the replacement characters.

4 Select **Replace All** to replace all occurrences of the characters.

Activity 5

1 Key in the letter given below, using standard letter layout and inserting the current date automatically
2 Use automatic replacement to change the price quoted from £90 to £150
3 Save as **UNIT6-4.DOC** and print one copy

Today's date

Mr and Mrs C Bates
6 Milwood Road
GILLINGHAM
KENT
ME7 5LN

Dear Mr and Mrs Bates

Thank you for your enquiry.

I have a special offer on 3-day breaks at the moment at £90 per person. This includes a double room with bath, breakfast and evening meal.

I can also offer you deluxe accommodation on 2-day breaks, half board, at the special price of £90 per person. In addition to a double room with bath, a sitting room is included.

These advantageous offers at £90 per person are for a limited time only and are proving very popular.

I shall look forward to hearing from you.

Yours sincerely

Paul Colicos
Manager

Many organisations send out letters which are repetitive and set up WP libraries with standard paragraphs.

Activity 6

1 The following are a selection of paragraphs from the WP library of a bank, set up to enable the automatic composition of repetitive letters
2 Set up each paragraph as a glossary item, without the numbers, naming them **PARA1**, **PARA2**, etc
3 So that you have a complete list of them, number them and print out for reference
4 Compose a letter to Mrs N Turner, 36 The Willows, High Wycombe, Bucks, HP13 7TB, using today's date and paragraphs 4 and 10. Print one copy
5 Compose a letter to Mr A Watts, 115 Green Street, High Wycombe, Bucks, HP10 3HW, using today's date and paragraphs 6 and 9. Print one copy

---

Standard Paragraphs

1 I have noticed that your account is slightly overdrawn and, although cheques are still being processed, this situation cannot be allowed to continue.

2 I regret that your account is very much overdrawn and, in these circumstances, no more cheques can be honoured.

3 I regret that you have suffered some embarrassment because your cheques could not be honoured. Your account is very much overdrawn and this matter was called to your attention. I am afraid that, unless there is a considerable cash injection to the account, cheques cannot be processed.

4 I regret that you were charged for safe custody in your last statement although you have no documents in our custody. The charges will be reimbursed in your next statement.

5 It has come to my attention that you are maintaining quite a large balance in your current account. I think it would be to your advantage to change over to an interest cheque account.

6 There have been one or two problems with your account. It would be advantageous if we met to discuss the situation.

7 I wonder if you are aware that we offer a financial advice service. If you are interested in investing your money for the very best return, please make an appointment to see our financial advisor, Mr S Walters. He will be pleased to assist you and, of course, there is no obligation to take his advice.

8 I regret that you have not been satisfied with our service and I think that a full discussion would be of benefit.

9 I should be grateful if you would make an appointment to see me. Please ring my secretary for a mutually convenient date.

10 I regret any inconvenience which has been caused and can assure you that this mistake will not happen again.

1 Storing standard paragraphs for legal documents

2 Storing words and phrases you use frequently, or have difficulty in remembering, or find difficult to spell

3 Saving typing

Problem solving

• *All occurrences of a word have been changed, instead of only some which you wanted to choose.*

When you displayed the Replace dialog box, you selected **Replace All** instead of **Find Next**. Select **Replace** from the **Edit** menu again and replace the new word with the old one. Then selectively replace the word again.

• *You have numbers for the paragraphs in your letter in Activity 6.*

You used the numbers, as well as the paragraphs to be saved, and highlighted them for the glossary. You will have to set up your glossary items again, without the numbers, to use them in the future. To correct your letter, remove the numbers by deleting or, if you used the Numbering button from the ribbon, highlight the paragraphs and select **Bullets and Numbering** from the **Tools** menu. Click on **Numbered List** and then select **Remove** to get rid of the numbers.

• *You have not succeeded in keying in the characters or words which are to be used for replacement.*

You may have pressed **Return** after keying the characters which are to be replaced. You should not press **Return** to terminate input; instead you should use the mouse to reposition the cursor in the next box into which you wish to enter information. Go through the whole replacement process again, using the mouse rather than the **Return** key.

• *You have the wrong menu on screen.*

Move the mouse outside the menu and click the mouse button. The menu will disappear and your cursor will be within the document again.

• *You have an unwanted dialog box on screen.*

Select the **Cancel** box to remove the dialog box.

• *You have a warning message on screen and you cannot carry on word processing.*

You cannot carry on until you have dealt with the message. Read the message and then select **OK** in the box containing the message. It will disappear and you can carry on. Make sure you follow any instructions given in the message.

Unit 7

Personal letters

Overview Personal letters use a similar format to business letters, but with the addition of the writer's home address on the right hand side at the top. There is a good deal of standard information which can be set up to use as a template for all future letters.

Existing skills
- Enhancing text - Unit 3
- Generating the date automatically - Unit 6

New skills
- Setting tabs
- Setting up a template
- Displaying the ruler
- Saving a file with a new name

Important When setting tabs, you need to display the ruler, so that you can see where the tabs are.

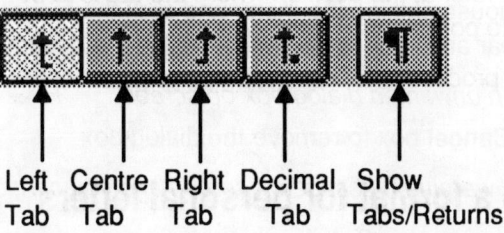

Left   Centre   Right   Decimal   Show
Tab   Tab   Tab   Tab   Tabs/Returns

TYPE OF TAB	HOW TYPING APPEARS ON SCREEN AND PAPER
Left	Begins at the set tab position and continues normally
Centre	Is centred on the tab position as you type
Right	Ends at the tab position, so typing moves to the right
Decimal	Numbers are positioned with the decimal point at the tab

7.1 Displaying the ruler

The tabs and margins ruler is not necessarily displayed on screen, but it is useful to be able to see it, if you are going to make any changes.

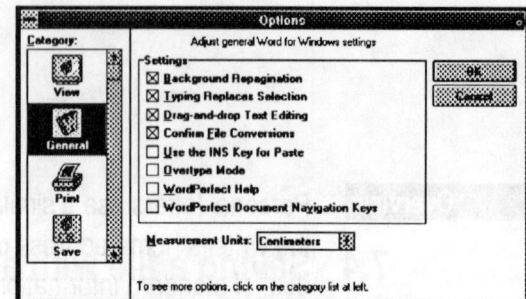

1 If the ruler is not displayed, select **Ruler** from the **View** menu.

2 You may find that Points or Picas, printers' measures, are used for measurement. If so, select **Options** from the **Tools** menu to display the **Options** dialog box.

3 Click on the arrow in the **Measurements** box to display the alternative measuring systems, and choose Centimetres or Inches, as you prefer.

7.2 Setting tabs

By default, tabs are set at 1/2" intervals. For many purposes, this will be acceptable, but sometimes you want different or fewer tabs

1 With the cursor at the beginning of the file, before you key in your text, select the button for the tab style you require from the ribbon.

2 Click on the ruler at the position where the tab is to be. You can drag it with the mouse to position it exactly.

3 Repeat this procedure for each tab you require.

7.3 Setting up a format for personal letters

1 Set a tab at about 4.5" (10.5 cm) from the left margin, ie 1.5" (4 cm) from the right margin, to use for the address. Set the font to italics (Italic).

2 Type in your home address, remembering to press the **Tab** key for each line, so that the address is at the right hand side.

3 Insert the date automatically.

1 Clear the screen and display the ruler, if necessary
2 Check that the **Return** button ¶ is pressed. If not select it to show **Return** and **Tab** characters
3 Set a tab at 4.5" and choose italics
4 Complete the format as shown below and save as **UNIT7-1.DOC**

55 Garfield Street
Teddington
Middlesex
TW11 9PX

Today's date

7.4 Saving a file with a new name

1 Open an existing file.

2 Edit the text as required and then select **Save As** from the **File** menu.

3 Key in your new file name in the dialog box displayed and press **Return**. The file will be saved with the new name.

7.5 Using the personal letter format

1 Load up the file which holds the letter format.

2 Complete the letter and save with a new name, so that the letter format is still saved on disc.

3 Make any necessary corrections, save again and print.

1 Open the personal letter format stored as **UNIT7-1.DOC**
2 Change the address given to your own, to make a template for your own letters
3 If you have a longer line in your address than those used in the example, then set a new tab nearer to the left margin to accommodate this line. Alternatively, you may want to make the tab setting nearer the right margin, if you have very short lines
4 Save as **PERS-LET.DOC** and print one copy for reference

1 Load up the personal letter format stored as **UNIT7-1.DOC**
2 Complete the letter shown below, making sure that all the text is in italic style
3 Save as **UNIT7-2.DOC** and print one copy

55 Garfield Street
Teddington
Middlesex
TW11 9PX

Today's date

Mr & Mrs T Meldrum
Hollytree Cottage
Torrington
North Devon
EX11 5HT

Dear Babs and Tom

Thank you so much for a lovely weekend. I thoroughly enjoyed the fresh country air and the food was delicious, as always.

I had a good journey back and found the cat in good shape, thanks to my neighbour.

I shall look forward to seeing you next month at the Townsends'.

With best wishes

Problem solving
- *The address is not lined up correctly.*

  You did not press the Tab key at the beginning of each line. Check that there is a tab code on each line. Delete any extra ones, or insert any which are missing.

- *You have to press the Tab key more than once to move to the position for the address.*

  You have not set up the new tab setting correctly. Select the whole address and set the tab again.

- *You have more tabs than you require in some paragraphs.*

  Tabs are a feature of a paragraph, rather than the whole document, unless set before keying anything at all. Select the paragraph which has the extra tab, then select **Tabs** from the **Format** menu and click on **Clear All**.

Unit 8

Simple tables

Overview
Most column work can be displayed by setting up tabs as part of the page layout, but a more powerful and flexible method is to use tables. Using these, you will be able to change the column settings easily.

Existing skills
- Centring text on entry - Unit 3
- Emboldening text - Unit 3

New skills
- Creating a table
- Editing a table
- Totalling values in a table

Important
Tables should be used in preference to tabs, as they are much more powerful, and considerably easier to change to accommodate amendments and insertions. They can also have their shape altered to fit the space available.

Columns

Rows

Selected row

8.1 Creating a table

A table is specified by the number of columns and rows it has. When you define a new table, the number of columns you specify will set the column width, as the whole table will fill the space between margins.

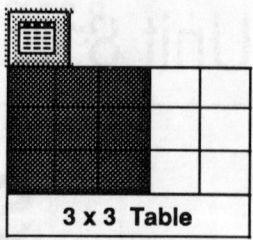

3 x 3 Table

1 Click on **Table** in the menu bar to display the **Table** menu. If there is not a tick beside **Gridlines**, then select it to tick it. This will make gridlines visible in any table you create.

2 Move your cursor to the position in the text where your table is to begin.

3 Click the mouse on the **Table** button from the toolbar and hold down the mouse button. A grid will be displayed at the pointer.

4 Drag the mouse to set the grid to the number of rows and columns you want. Release the mouse button to set the size.

5 A grid with the specified number of columns and rows will be displayed on screen. Each cell should have gridlines and an insertion point displayed.

6 Use the cursor or mouse to select each cell and type in its contents, using the Tab and cursor keys to move between cells.

Important If you find controlling the mouse difficult, then you may find it easier to select **Insert Table** from the **Table** menu and set the number of columns and rows with this dialog box.

Activity 1

1 If necessary, clear the screen and key in the title *A Demonstration Table* on the first line
2 With the cursor on the next line, create a table with 7 rows and 4 columns
3 Enter the information given below in the table cells as shown. You will notice that some cells will increase in height to fit the text
4 Save the title and table as **UNIT8-1.DOC**
5 Print a copy. The gridlines will not be printed

VILLAGE HALL	SCHEME	COST	RECOMMENDATIONS
		£	£
Briarwood	New heating system		
	New kitchen units	6,500.00	3,250.00
Basilford	Replace flat roof		
	Replace ceiling	9,420.00	5,537.00
Deshall	Purchase of land	9,500.00	2,600.00

8.2 Changing column width

1 Move the cursor onto a vertical gridline, until the cursor changes to a double headed horizontal arrow.

2 Drag the gridline to widen or narrow the column the required amount. This will affect all columns to the right of it.

Important As the column width is set initially to fill the space between the margins, it is best to narrow a column first, to make space available to widen columns.

8.3 Joining and splitting cells

If text is too wide to fit in one cell, as will often be the case with headings, you can combine adjacent cells to display the text, without having to change the width or height of a complete column or row. This is called merging. Splitting cells means making them into individual cells again.

1 Highlight the cells which are to be joined and select **Merge cells** from the **Table** menu.

2 The cells are now one combined cell.

3 To split a previously merged cell, move the cursor to it and select **Split cells** from the **Table** menu.

Activity 2

1 Set up a table with 6 columns and 9 rows for the information given below
2 Join all the cells in the first row, before typing in the heading, centred and emboldened, as shown. Use the normal methods for this, ie selecting buttons on the toolbar
3 Key in the remaining cells, emboldening as shown
4 Narrow all columns except the second, then widen the second column, as shown below
5 Preview to check display, save as **UNIT8-2.DOC** and print

EXPENSES					
Month	**Details**	**Total**	**Miles**	**Misc**	**VAT**
March	150 miles @ 52.8p	79.20	79.20		
March	Photocopying	8.18		6.96	1.22
March	Printer ribbons	21.86		18.61	3.25
March	Parcel	0.28		0.28	
March	Taxi	10.00	10.00		
March	Trade booklet	0.50		0.50	

8.4 Inserting rows and columns

1 Move the cursor to the position where a row or column is to be inserted.

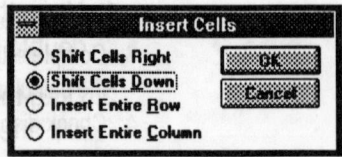

2 Select **Insert cells** from the **Table** menu to display the **Insert Cells** dialog box.

3 Highlight either **Insert Entire Row** or **Insert Entire Column** and select **OK**. A blank row or column will be inserted at the cursor position.

8.5 Deleting a column

1 Select the column (click the right mouse button anywhere in the column) which is to be deleted.

2 Select **Delete Columns** from the **Table** menu to delete the column.

Activity 3

1 Load up the file **UNIT8-1.DOC** which contains the table created in Activity 1
2 Insert a row for the heading, embolden and centre as shown
3 Adjust the column widths to fit the text, as shown
4 Preview, save with the same name and print

VILLAGE HALL GRANT APPLICATIONS			
VILLAGE HALL	SCHEME	COST	RECOMMENDATIONS
		£	£
Briarwood	New heating system		
	New kitchen units	6,500.00	3,250.00
Basilford	Replace flat roof		
	Replace ceiling	9,420.00	5,537.00
Deshall	Purchase of land	9,500.00	2,600.00

8.6 Adding a column of figures

1 Select the column or row (click the left mouse button in the left margin beside the row) which is to be totalled,

2 Select **Calculate** from the **Tools** menu. The total of all the numbers in the row or column, ignoring all text, will be saved to the clipboard.

3 Select the cell where the total is to be displayed and select the **Paste** button from the toolbar to paste in the result.

1 Open the file **UNIT8-2.DOC**, which contains a table
2 Insert an additional row at the top of the table for the main title, joining the cells before entering the title, centred and emboldened
3 Complete the bottom row with the title, total the third column automatically and then apply the calculation to the remaining columns
4 Check display, save again and print

SALES DEPARTMENT					
EXPENSES					
Month	**Details**	**Total**	**Miles**	**Misc**	**VAT**
March	150 miles @ 52.8p	79.20	79.20		
March	Photocopying	8.18		6.96	1.22
March	Printer ribbons	21.86		18.61	3.25
March	Parcel	0.28		0.28	
March	Taxi	10.00	10.00		
March	Trade booklet	0.50		0.50	
	Total	120.02	89.20	26.35	4.47

8.7 Moving rows to new positions

1 Select the row, using the left mouse button in the margin.

2 Click and hold down the left mouse button in the highlighting and drag to the new position. Release the button.

1 Open the file **UNIT8-2.DOC** again
2 Exchange the first two heading rows by moving the first one into a new position, as shown
3 Save with the same name

EXPENSES					
PRODUCTION DEPARTMENT					
Month	**Details**	**Total**	**Miles**	**Misc**	**VAT**
March	150 miles @ 52.8p	79.20	79.20		
March	Photocopying	8.18		6.96	1.22
March	Printer ribbons	21.86		18.61	3.25
March	Parcel	0.28		0.28	
March	Taxi	10.00	10.00		
March	Trade booklet	0.50		0.50	
	Total	120.02	89.20	26.35	4.47

1 Quotations

2 Curriculum Vitae (*see* Unit 9)

3 Invoices (*see* Unit 11)

Problem solving • *Some of the rows are double sized.*

You have pressed **Return** at the end of an entry, instead of using **Tab** or the pointer to move to the next cell. Move the cursor to the cell and delete the **Return** character.

• *You cannot widen a column to fit its contents.*

You have not first narrowed a column, so your table fills the whole page. Follow the procedure to narrow a column to make some space, then try again.

• *You have changed one of the figures in your table, but the column total is still the same as before.*

Totals are not automatically recalculated when you change a value in a table. Delete the total, select the column again and then use **Tools Calculate** to perform the calculation again.

• *You cannot drag a column to a new position.*

You have clicked the mouse button with the pointer outside the highlighted column, which deselects it. Highlight the column and try again. Successful dragging depends only on mouse operation.

• *You cannot carry out the calculation.*

You can perform calculations only if the appropriate figures are highlighted. Highlight them and try again.

• *You have difficulty in manipulating your table because you cannot see where the cells begin and end.*

You did not check that the **Gridlines** option was ticked in the **Table** menu. Do so now and the gridlines will be displayed, giving you a clear view of where the cells are.

Unit 9

Itineraries and CVs

Some complicated tabulated work, which would be difficult using special tabs, can be accomplished with multi-line tables. This is particularly useful for displays which include side headings. It is always worth considering, when you are setting tabs, whether using a table would be more appropriate.

Existing skills
- Increasing the size of text - Unit 4
- Creating a table - Unit 8
- Editing a table - Unit 8

New skills
- Using lines in tables
- Using multi-line tables

The right line is wide for emphasis	Very long titles need several lines of text		

9.1 Adding borders to a table

1 Highlight all the cells to which you wish to add a border.

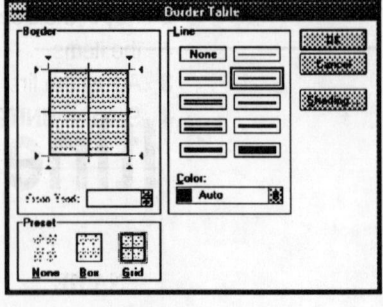

2 Select **Border** from the **Format** menu to display the **Border Table** dialogue box.

3 Select one of the 3 preset border formats from the bottom of the box, or choose for each possible line by clicking on the diagram.

4 Choose the width of line you want and then click on **OK**.

9.2 Multi-line rows in a table

1 Key in the first line of the entry in a cell and press **Return**.

2 The row height will increase to fit in another line of text.

3 Key in the second and subsequent lines in the same cell.

Activity 1

1 Clear the screen, if necessary, and set up a table with 3 columns and 11 rows to contain the itinerary shown below, allowing a row for each item, however long, and one blank row between each item. *The row numbers are to show you where each entry is to go*

2 Merge the cells in the first row for the title. Add a border round the whole table, as shown, make any adjustments to column widths needed and embolden where appropriate

3 Save as **UNIT9-1.DOC** and print

	Depart	Arrive	Details
1	**TRAVEL ITINERARY - Monday 6 April**		
2			
3	**Depart**	**Arrive**	**Details**
4			
5	0915	1100	London to Leicester
6			
7		1115	Patel's Wholesalers, 112 High Street Tel: 0509 780023
8			
9	1400	1530	Nottm - see Mr Simpson, 59 Market Street Tel: 0509 773421
10			
11	1730	1800	Grand Hotel, Shire Street Tel: 0509 708451

1   Set up a 2 column table to hold the CV given below, allowing one row for each item
2   Key in the side headings, then each entry, ending in an extra Return to give space between the items
3   Adjust the first column to fit the longest side heading
4   Save as **UNIT9-2.DOC** and print

CURRICULUM VITAE

NAME	Andrew Gere
ADDRESS	77 Thorn Road
	Bridlington
	N Humberside
	YO14 3BT
TELEPHONE	0262 632711
MARITAL STATUS	Single
NATIONALITY	British
EDUCATION	1983-85 King Edward School, Bradford
	1985-87 Barside Technical College,
	Bradford
QUALIFICATIONS	GCSE in English, Geography, History,
	Mathematics and Music
	BTEC National Diploma in Business Studies
WORK EXPERIENCE	1987 to present
	Sales Executive with Barside Cars
HOBBIES/INTERESTS	Badminton, Football, Music
REFEREES	Mr N I Preedon, BSc, MEd, FRSA
	Principal
	Barside Technical College
	BRADFORD BD1 9RH
	Telephone: 0274 800432
	Ms A Line
	Managing Director
	Barside Cars
	Cliff Road
	BRADFORD BD9 7CR
	Telephone: 0274 811045

Further uses

1 Any programme which can be split into columns, such as one for a concert or show

2 Handbills with side headings

3 Timetables

4 Weekly diaries

Problem solving

• *There are no gaps between a piece of text and the next side heading.*

You have not pressed **Return** at the end of the text. Select the cell, move to the end of the text and press **Return**.

• *There are some lines in the wrong places in your table.*

You did not mark the whole table as a block before formatting the borders. Mark the block again and follow the procedure for making borders to change your choices, removing the lines you do not want from the sample in the dialog box, and then putting in the extra ones you do want.

• *The heading in Activity 1 is on two lines, rather than on one as in the sample.*

You did not merge the cells in the first row before keying in the heading. Merge the cells and rekey, if necessary.

• *Your line ends are not the same as in the samples.*

Your table is considerably wider than the ones shown, as you are using A4 paper. Narrow the columns to reflect the display given.

• *Not all the headings are emboldened.*

Highlight the cells which are not emboldened and select the **Bold** button from the toolbar.

Unit 10

Memos

An organisation will sometimes have special memo stationery, with a printed heading. Another option is to set up a standard heading using a template file. This can then be used whenever a memo is to be keyed in.

- Centring text - Unit 3
- Enhancing text - Unit 3
- Setting tabs - Unit 7
- Generating the date automatically - Unit 6

- Using End key to move cursor

Important   Once you have set up a template, you should be careful not to alter the original version. You should *Write protect* it to be sure of this.

10.1 Setting up a memo template

1 Clear the screen, if necessary.

2 Set tabs at 0.25" and 1.5".

3 Key in the main heading for your memo, using centred bold large text and double spaced letters.

4 Enter the standard side headings, separated by blank lines.

5 Check carefully, save and print.

1 Clear the screen, if necessary
2 Key in the following text to a new file, pressing the **Tab** key after each side heading
3 Embolden and centre as shown
4 Save to disk as file **MEMO.DOC**

MEMORANDUM

Date:

To:

From:

Subject:

10.2 Using the memo template

1 Open the file which contains the memo template.

2 Save the file with a new name, so that the template is left unchanged.

3 Edit this file by adding the details for the particular memo you want to send, using the **End** key to move the cursor to the end of the line for each side heading.

4 Generate the date automatically.

5 Preview the file, to check the display.

6 Save and print.

Activity 2

1. Load up the file **MEMO.DOC**
2. Key in the memo given below
3. Save it as the file **UNIT10-1.DOC** and print

M E M O R A N D U M

Date: Today's date

To: All Staff

From: Manager

Subject: Stocktaking

Stocktaking will take place next Sunday, commencing at 1630 hours.   It is expected that all staff will take part. Normal Sunday overtime rates will apply or time off in lieu may be arranged with your Supervisor.

Activity 3

1. Load up the file **MEMO.DOC**
2. Key in the memo given below
3. Save it as the file **UNIT10-2.DOC** and print

M E M O R A N D U M

Date: Today's date

To: All Supervisors

From: Manager

Subject: Official Opening

There will be a meeting in my office next Monday morning at 8.30 am in connection with the official opening. Please arrange your duties so that you will be able to attend. The meeting should not take more that half an hour.

---

1 Template files may be set up for any standard documents eg letters, reports, contracts

2 It is useful to create a template with a frequently used letter heading as in an organisation's details or a personal address

Problem solving • *You have saved the edited version of the memo using* **Save** *instead of* **Save As***, so it has the same name as before, overwriting the original.*

If you have followed the instructions correctly in Preparing to Use Word for Windows, you will have a backup copy of the memo template called **MEMO.BAK** on disk. You can rename it and use it again, using the Windows File Manager.

• *You do not know how to write protect a file to prevent the problem listed above.*

You should use the Windows File Manager to do this. Open the Windows File Manager and highlight the appropriate file. Then select **Change Attributes** (Windows version 3.0) *or* **Properties** (Windows version 3.1) from the **File** menu and click on the **Read Only** box. The file cannot then be saved, only read in and saved with a different name.

Unit 11

Invoices

Overview When you are producing invoices and other documents which involve numbers, you can use the mathematical features of Word for Windows tables to do the calculations. You might also find it useful to use any additional fonts your printer can produce to make an attractive heading.

Existing skills
- Changing text size - Unit 4
- Setting up and editing a table - Unit 8
- Totalling values in a table - Unit 8
- Using lines in tables - Unit 9

New skills
- Changing fonts
- Using formulae in tables

Important A font is a typeface, which can be produced in a number of point sizes [72 points = 1"] and a number of weights, i e bold, medium and light. As with type sizes, the ability to print out some fonts will depend on the capabilities of your printer. A few examples are given below.

TYPE OF FONT	NAME	FEATURES
Sans Serif	Helvetica/Swiss	Plain characters with no extra strokes
Serif	Times Roman	Small characters with extra strokes
Monospaced	Courier	All characters are the same width
Script	*Chancery*	Handwritten joined letter style

11.1 Changing fonts ▕ Times New Roman ▕▼▏

1 Before entering text, or after highlighting existing text, click on the arrow beside the currently selected font name to display a complete list of fonts available.

2 Select a font from the list and continue keying in text until a different font is required.

Activity 1

1 Clear the screen and key in text in each font you have on your printer. Choose a sans serif font, if available, closest in appearance to the Helvetica used in the invoice heading

2 Select **New** from the **File** menu to clear the screen

3 Key in the invoice heading given below, following the display and alignment, and using the sans serif font you have chosen for the heading

4 Save as **INVOICE.DOC** to use as an invoice template, preview and print

---

I N V O I C E No **0000**

K B BROWN (CONTRACTORS) LTD

BUILDING AND CIVIL ENGINEERS
Station Close
Nottingham   Telephone: 0602 894571
NG1 7CS   Fax: 0602 893156

Date:
Customer name

VAT NO: 233 4532 21

Activity 2

1 Load up **INVOICE.TMP** saved in Activity 1, insert a blank line before the VAT number and move the cursor there

2 Set up a 2 column, 3 row table for the values shown on the next page. Enter the text and use calculation to give the final total

3 Enter top and bottom lines for the bottom right cell, as shown

4 Save as **UNIT11-1.DOC** and print one copy

```
To works completed in accordance with
your letter dated 1 August

            VAT @ 17.5%                    _____

            TOTAL                          _____
```

---

1 Load up **UNIT11-1.DOC**
2 Enter the details for the invoice shown below, including the price and VAT, following the display given
3 Use **Tools Calculate** to perform the calculation for the total price
4 Check the display, save and print one copy

INVOICE No **7918**

K B BROWN (CONTRACTORS) LTD

BUILDING AND CIVIL ENGINEERS
Station Close
Nottingham   Telephone: 0602 894571
NG1 7CS   Fax: 0602 893156

10 October 19..

Mr L Tomlins
307 Upperton Road
NOTTINGHAM
NG10 9UR

New Retaining Wall, Hales Fields, Nottingham

To works completed in accordance with   2122.00
your letter dated 1 August

                    VAT @ 17.5%   371.35
                                                    ─────────────
                    TOTAL   2493.35

VAT NO: 233 4532 21

11.2 Using formulae in tables

You have already used calculation to add columns of figures in Activity 3. As well as this special function, you can use general formulae in tables, similar to those used in simple spreadsheets.

The cells in a table are labelled in exactly the same way as some spreadsheets for reference in formulae, by row and column number, eg r3c2 as shown.

Column letters

	c1	c2	c3	c4
r1				
r2				
r3		Cell r3c2		
r4				
r5				
r6				

Row numbers

1 Create the table, key in the text and figures and adjust the column widths to display the information sensibly.

2 Move the cursor to the cell in which the formula is to be entered, ie the one in which the *answer* to the calculation is to be displayed.

3 Select **Field** from the **Insert** menu to display the **Field** dialog box.

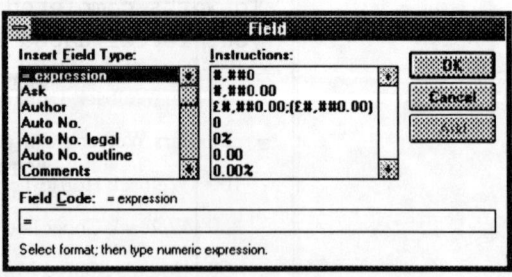

4 Enter the expression in the box indicated, using cell references and arithmetic operations, eg formula **SUM([r1c1:r1c2])** entered into cell r1c3 would add the contents of r1c1 and r1c2 and put the answer in cell r1c3.

Important In calculations which use all entries in one row, you can leave out the column number, eg r3 means all the cells in row 3.

1 Load up the file **UNIT11-1.DOC**, the invoice saved in Activity 3
2 Edit the heading to use it for the invoice below, which has the same layout
3 Save as file **UNIT11-2.DOC**
4 Delete the table and set up instead one with 4 columns and 10 rows
5 Enter in the table the Number, Item and Unit Price for each item. Then insert a field containing the formula **product([r2c1],[r2c3])** in the final column for the first item
6 Repeat the formula for the remaining 4 items, then total the column automatically
7 Remove and set gridlines as shown
8 Save and print

INVOICE No **0873**

WELBACK WHOLESALE LTD

112 Forest Road
BRADFORD
W Yorkshire
BD1 8HR

Telephone: 0274 839912
Fax: 0274 856411

Today's date

Mr D Moyer
The Corner Shop
Haworth
W Yorkshire
BD10 5CH

No	Item	Unit Price	Total Price
5	Jar Welback Drinking Chocolate 124 gm	1.18	5.90
20	Jars Welback Coffee Granules 100 gm	1.49	29.80
100	Welback House Tea Bags 60's	1.69	169.00
50	Welback Chocolate Chip Cookies 100 gm	0.34	17.00
50	Hounds Malted Milk 125 gm	0.64	32.00
	TOTAL	£	253.70

5% Cash Discount for payment on delivery

VAT Registered No 134 6723 43

1 Any letter which includes calculations

2 Quotations

3 Simple estimates

• *When you enter the formula for a calculation, you get the answer 0.00.*

You have not yet entered values in all the cells you are using in the calculation. Enter the values and recalculate.

• *The answer to a calculation is different to that shown.*

You may have changed a figure since you entered the calculation. Select function key **F9** to recalculate. If this does not solve the problem, you may have entered a formula wrongly. Select **Field Codes** from the **View** menu to display the expression you entered. Check the formula and edit it, if necessary.

• *The tables have borders right round them, which looks strange in the middle of an invoice.*

Remove all borders and put in new ones only where required, by selecting a cell or blocks of cells which need borders on the same side of them.

• *The fonts and text sizes you have chosen do not look much like the samples.*

Your fonts depend entirely on the printer you are using. The ones shown are Postscript fonts produced on a laser printer. On a matrix printer with Windows 3.0, your choices may be much more limited. Select some alternative fonts and preview them to choose the ones you like best.

• *When you have entered your formula for total price in Activity 4, the field displays the message 'Syntax error'.*

You have typed the formula incorrectly; most likely you have omitted a bracket. The brackets are used as follows:

TYPE	PRINTED	USE
Square brackets	[ ]	placed either side of cell name
Round brackets	( )	contains the cells to be used for the function
Braces	{ }	put in automatically by Word to contain a field
Comma	,	placed between cell names in a list

Your field should look exactly like the sample below, including spacing. Select **Field codes** from the **View** menu to display your expression and edit it. Then select the option again to display the answer and press **F9** to update the calculation.

$$\{= \mathrm{Product}([r2c1],[r2c3])\}$$

Unit 12

Meeting notices and agendas

Overview   Not all text fits neatly on to the A4 or standard continuous stationery you have been using so far. You can choose alternative page and paper sizes very easily, and change between them to suit the job. You can also customise paper size, margins and a number of other page layout features through the Page Setup command.

Existing skills
- Copying blocks of text - Unit 2
- Enhancing text - Unit 3
- Changing text size - Unit 4
- Using templates - Unit 7
- Setting tabs - Unit 7

New skills
- Changing page and paper size
- Setting up special page sizes
- Combining two files

Important   If you change page size, you will probably need to change the left and right margins as well. This is particularly important if you choose smaller paper, where the default margins will be much too large.

12.1 Selecting a new paper size

Paper sizes are a general feature, not related to any particular document. Once a new size has been chosen or created, it can be set as the default size.

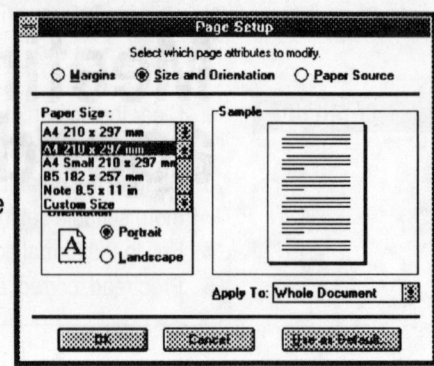

1 Select **Page Setup** from the **Format** menu to display the **Page Setup** dialog box.

2 Select the **Size and Orientation** radio button to display the appropriate options.

3 Click on the arrow at the edge of the **Paper Size** box to display the available options for paper size. This will vary according to your printer.

4 If the size you want is displayed, select it. If not, select **Custom Size** and key in the width and height you want.

5 Click **Use as Default** and then **Yes** in the dialog box displayed, *only* if you want all future documents to have the new paper size.

6 Select the **Margins** radio button and key in new margins, if necessary. Click **OK** to exit to the text.

Activity 1

1 If you have already completed Unit 10 and so have **MEMO.DOC** saved on disk, open it
or
If the file is not on disk, key in the memo format shown below, with a tab set at 1.5"

2 Set up a custom page size with the A5 measurements of 5.83" x 8.27"[14.83 x 21 cm]. *You can print A5 documents on A4 or standard 11" continuous paper for practice*

3 Save the template again, with the same name

MEMORANDUM

Date:

To:

From:

Subject:

12.2 Notices of meeting

Notices for meetings are sent out in advance by the Secretary to those entitled to attend. They may be formal or informal, but must give the minimum information of date, time and venue.

Activity 2

1 Clear the screen, if necessary
2 Change the default paper size to A5, as set up in Activity 1
3 Change the default left and right margins to 0.75" (2 cm) and 0.5" [1.3 cm] respectively, more suitable settings for A5 paper
4 Key in the formal notice of meeting shown below, keeping to the given display
5 Proofread, correct any mistakes, save as **UNIT12-1.DOC** and print one copy

---

PARISH OF WILFORD ON THE WOLDS

NOTICE OF MEETING OF THE PARISH COUNCIL

Dear Sir/Madam

There will be a meeting of the Parish Council at Wilford Village Hall on Monday, 9 March at 7.30 pm.

Dated Monday 2 March

K N Moyse
Clerk of the Parish Council

Activity 3

1 Clear the screen and key in the formal notice of AGM given below, using enhancements as shown
2 Add 3 extra blank lines at the end of the notice
3 Copy and paste the whole notice, with the blank lines, twice more on to the page
4 Preview to check the display and add any extra blank lines needed
5 Save as **UNIT12-2.DOC** and print one copy

Formal notice of AGM

THE COUNTRYSIDE CONSERVATION ASSOCIATION

The Annual General Meeting of the Countryside Conservation Association will be held at the Association Head Office, Barton House, Connaught Place, Teddington, Middlesex, on Thursday, 31 March at 1400 hours.

---

1 Retrieve the memo template saved as **MEMO.DOC** in Activity 1
2 Use it to produce the informal notice of meeting shown below, using tab to line up the items in the heading and generating the date automatically
3 Save as **UNIT12-3.DOC**

M E M O R A N D U M

Date: *Today's date*

To: Midlands Sales Staff

From: Sales Director (Midlands)

Subject: Sales Meeting

There will be a meeting of all Midlands sales staff at Soar House, New Road, Leicester, on Wednesday, 12 March, at 1000 hours.

12.3 Agenda layout

There is a standard layout for a meeting agenda, which is made up of standard items of business, 1-3, 9 and 10 in the sample, together with additional items specific to the particular organisation and meeting. It is, therefore, worth having an agenda template.

A G E N D A

1 Apologies
2 Minutes of last meeting
3 Matters arising
4)
5)
6) Specific subjects
7)
8)
9 Any other business
10 Date and time of next meeting

1 Clear the screen, if necessary, and choose paper size A4 or 11" continuous, depending on your printer

2 Check your margins and change them to 1" (2.5 cm) either side, if necessary

3 Key in the agenda template, check and save as **AGENDA.DOC**

A G E N D A

1 Apologies
2 Minutes of last meeting
3 Matters arising
4
5
6
7
8
9 Any other business
10 Date and time of next meeting

12.4 Combining two files

When you want 2 existing files to be joined together to form one document, which flows on continuously, you can combine them very easily.

1 Open the first file in the usual way to display it on screen.

2 Move the cursor to the position in the document where the second file is to start, usually either at the beginning or end of the first file.

3 Select **File** from the **Insert** menu and select the second file from the **File** dialog box displayed. It will be read in, beginning at the cursor position.

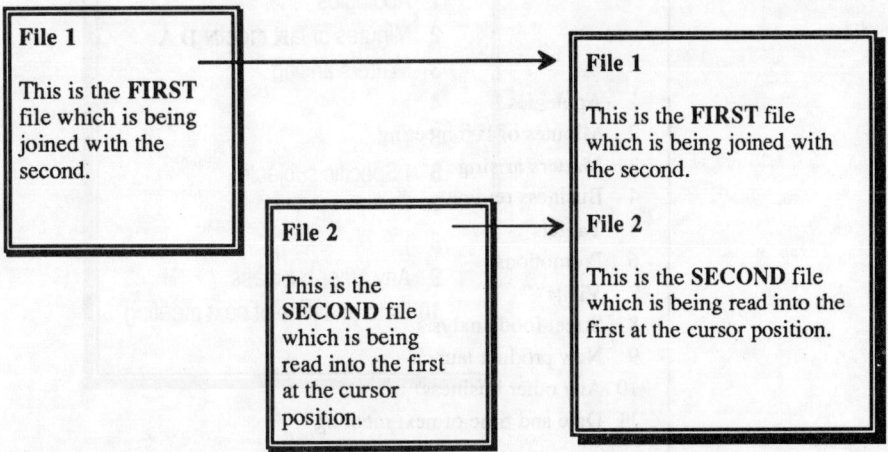

File 1

This is the **FIRST** file which is being joined with the second.

File 2

This is the **SECOND** file which is being read into the first at the cursor position.

File 1

This is the **FIRST** file which is being joined with the second.

File 2

This is the **SECOND** file which is being read into the first at the cursor position.

1 As a notice of meeting and the relevant agenda are usually sent out together, these 2 files can be combined to fit on one page

2 Open the agenda template saved as **AGENDA.DOC** in Activity 5 and complete it for a meeting of the Midland Sales Staff by adding the following items of business

> 4 Business review
> 5 Targets
> 6 Promotions
> 7 Visits
> 8 Street food analysis
> 9 New product launch

3 Save as **UNIT12-4.DOC**, ie a different name so that the template still exists to be used again

4 Read in the notice of meeting saved as **UNIT12-3.DOC** in Activity 4, to create a combined document

5 Check and preview, and select A4 or 11" continuous paper, depending on your printer

6 Save again and print

M E M O R A N D U M

Date: 5 March 19xx

To: Midlands Sales Staff

From: Sales Director (Midlands)

Subject: Sales Meeting

There will be a meeting of all Midlands sales staff at Soar House, New Road, Leicester, on Wednesday, 12 March, at 1000 hours.

A G E N D A

1 Apologies
2 Minutes of last meeting
3 Matters arising
4 Business review
5 Targets
6 Promotions
7 Visits
8 Street food analysis
9 New product launch
10 Any other business
11 Date and time of next meeting

---

1 Open the notice of AGM for the Countryside Conservation Association saved as **UNIT12-2.DOC** in Activity 3

2 Delete the second and third copies of the notice

3 Read in the agenda template saved as **AGENDA.DOC** in Activity 5 and complete it as shown in the sample below, by adding the following items of business:

    4 Chair's report
    5 Secretary's report
    6 Treasurer's report
    7 Election of Officers
    8 Schools' Conservation Programme

4 Save with a new name **UNIT12-4.DOC** and print one copy

Formal notice of AGM

THE COUNTRYSIDE CONSERVATION ASSOCIATION

The Annual General Meeting of the Countryside Conservation Association will be held at the Association Head Office, Barton House, Connaught Place, Teddington, Middlesex, on Thursday, 31 March 19xx at 1400 hours.

A G E N D A

1   Apologies
2   Minutes of last meeting
3   Matters arising
4   Chair's report
5   Secretary's report
6   Treasurer's report
7   Election of Officers
8   Schools' Conservation Programme
9   Any other business
10 Date and time of next meeting

---

1 Quotations

2 Extracting facts from another file for a letter

3 Laying out A5 booklets

• *The agenda and notice of meeting do not follow on from each other, but are interleaved.*

Your cursor was at the wrong place in your document when you retrieved the second file. Close the file, open the agenda again in its edited form, move your cursor to the end and insert the notice of meeting again.

• *Your paper size has not been used in previewing and printing a new file.*

You may have chosen the paper size only for the current document, rather than setting it as the default. Follow the procedure to change the page layout again.

• *You have more than one copy of the notice of AGM in Activity 7.*

You did not delete both the second and third copies of the notice of meeting before reading in the agenda file. Highlight all the unwanted text and delete it.

• *The agenda numbering is wrong in a combined file.*

You have used automatic numbering and have not cancelled it. Highlight each item in turn which does not need numbering and select **Bullets and Numbering** from the **Tools** menu to display the **Bullets and Numbering** dialog box. Click on **Numbered List** and select **Remove**. (*see* Unit 5)

• *Your text is printed the wrong way on the paper, ie landscape rather than portrait.*

You clicked on **Landscape** when changing paper size. Follow the procedure to change the page layout again and choose **Portrait**.

Unit 13

Chair's agenda

Overview In order to give a consistent look to your text, which is particularly important for documents which run over several pages, you can set up Styles. A style is a set of features which specify the appearance of any word or piece of text which has that style applied to it.

Existing skills
- Aligning text - Unit 4
- Changing text size - Unit 4
- Using tables - Unit 8

New skills
- Creating styles
- Saving and retrieving style files
- Converting text to tables

Important Possible styles depend entirely on your printer. Laser printers, and any printer being used with Windows, will provide a range of fonts measured in points (72 points = 1 inch). Twelve cpi (Elite typing) is approximately the same size as 10 point, which will give you an idea of the size to use.

The following features are usually set in styles:

- Font type and size
- Appearance ie underlining, emboldening, etc
- Alignment

Styles also need a name which is used for selection. The name should be chosen to prompt its use, eg Heading, Side heading, List.

13.1 Applying existing styles

Whenever you open a new or existing file, you use a template which has a set of styles. So far you have been using the **Normal** default template file and the default style **Normal**, which usually gives Times New Roman 10 point.

1 Click on the arrow beside the style name box to display the style options available.

2 Select a style and then key in the text or, alternatively, select a paragraph of existing text and then select the style you want for it.

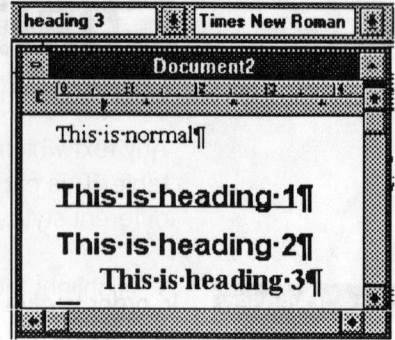

13.2 Creating a new style

1 Highlight a paragraph in your text and select the attributes you want for your style, ie font, text size, enhancement and alignment.

2 Select the style name box on the ribbon and key in the name of the new style, followed by pressing **Return**.

Activity 1

1 If you have already completed Unit 12 and so have **UNIT12-4.DOC** saved on disk, open it, display on screen and delete all but the numbered items. Insert blank lines as shown
or
If the file is not on disk, key in the agenda shown below, using automatic numbering

```
1   Apologies

2   Minutes of last meeting

3   Matters arising

4   Business Review

5   Targets

6   Promotions

7   Visits

8   Street food analysis

9   New product launch

10  Any other business

11  Date and time of next meeting
```

2 Create 3 styles as follows, with suitable descriptions
   Centre head - centred, sans serif 16 point, bold
   Side head - left justified, sans serif 12 point, bold
   Body text - left justified, serif 10 point
3 Save the file, with the styles, as **UNIT13-1.DOC**

13.3 Converting text to a table

Any text which is separated by tabs, commas or **Return**s can be made into a table. This can be useful in several circumstances, eg when you want to apply different styles to text on the same line.

1 Highlight the text which is to be converted and select **Convert Text to Table** from the **Table** menu. Widen columns to accommodate the text.

2 Insert any additional columns you need. If you need an extra column at the end, position the cursor just after the final column, select **Select Column** from the **Table** menu, followed by **Insert Columns** from the **Table** menu.

Activity 2
1 Open file **UNIT13-1.DOC** which was saved with its accompanying styles in Activity 1
2 Convert the numbers and agenda items to a table, insert 2 columns and add the comments to the agenda for the Chair, leaving 2 line spaces between items (for notes)
3 Apply Centre Head style to the edited heading, Side Heading style to the numbers and agenda items and Body text to the comments
4 Save the agenda and print

CHAIR'S AGENDA

1 Apologies	1 Tod Crisp/Helen Danvers
2 Minutes of last meeting	2 Sign
3 Matters arising	3 Present charts and graphs
4 Business Review	4 Tam Wyatt
5 Targets	
6 Promotions	6 Details from Kelly Jay
7 Visits	7 Individual reports
8 Street food analysis	8 Statistics
9 New product launch	9 Take samples 'Panther'
10 Any other business	
11 Date and time of next meeting	11 Allow one month - to be held in Nottingham

1 Reports (*see* Unit 17)

2 Newsletters (*see* Unit 21)

3 Any document which requires consistent display

• *Your text does not look like the samples*

You may just have a different set of fonts available. The samples were produced on a laser printer using Helvetica. Your sans serif font may look quite different.

• *The correct page size has not been used in printing the file.*

If you have not already completed Unit 12, you will not have set up a new page size. Follow the procedure given in Unit 12 to set a new page size.

• *When you converted your text to a table, the text appeared in vertical columns.*

The columns which have been created for you are very narrow, so they do not display the text properly. Widen the columns with the mouse to make room for the text.

• *When you converted your text to a table, the heading is centred only over the first column.*

You did not merge the columns in the first row. Do so now, to centre the heading over the whole table.

• *Not all the text is included in the table.*

You did not highlight all the text before conversion. Highlight the table and select **Convert Table to Text** from the **Table** menu. Then highlight **all** the text and convert it to a table again.

• *You cannot create a new style.*

You have not highlighted existing text before creating the new style. Highlight a paragraph or line and try again.

Unit 14

Minutes

Objectives

In all the units so far, the text has fitted neatly on to one page, either A4, 11" continuous stationery or A5. In reality, many documents take up more than one page. It is in formatting pages that word processing really comes into its own, as quite major changes can be accomplished with a few key strokes. To give consistency throughout a document and across similar documents within an institution, a standard page layout is adopted, for margins at each side and at the top and bottom, page size, numbering, fonts, heading styles and type sizes.

Existing skills

- Indenting paragraphs - Unit 5
- Generating the date automatically - Unit 6
- Setting tabs - Unit 7
- Using styles - Unit 13

New skills

- Setting up and editing headers and footers
- Numbering pages
- Printing selected pages
- Splitting pages at convenient points in text

Important

Headers and footers are lines of text which appear on every page, or on all even or odd pages, if you prefer. They usually contain items such as file names, date and time, chapter headings in books, and most usefully, page numbers.

Header in the header margin

Left margin

Page layout

Right margin

Footer   Page 1

14.1 Setting up a footer

A footer is text which appears in the bottom margin on every page, except perhaps the first one. It usually includes the page number, automatically generated by Word for Windows, but can also include any text of your choice; you may find the date and/or time and the file name useful.

1 Select **Normal** from the **View** menu, if necessary.

2 Select **Header/Footer** from the **View** menu, followed by **Footer** and **OK** to open the Footer pane on screen, with preset tabs for centring and right aligning within the current margins.

3 Position the cursor for the page number and click the **#** button to set it. Then enter any other text; date and time can also be set with buttons.

4 Click on the **Close** box to return to your text.

14.2 Setting up a header

A header is similar to a footer, but at the top of the page, and is more rarely used, except for chapter headings, and almost never on the first page. Headers are set up like footers, by selecting **Header** from the first dialog box.

Activity 1

1 If you have already completed Unit 13 and so have **UNIT13-1.DOC** saved on disk with its associated styles, open it, display on screen, convert to text and delete the comments
or
If the file is not on disk, set up the styles specified in Activity 1 of Unit 13. Key in the agenda shown below, applying Centre Head style to the heading and Side Heading style to the numbers and agenda items

2 Save as **UNIT14-1.DOC**

> ### A G E N D A
>
> 1 **Apologies**
> 2 **Minutes of last meeting**
> 3 **Matters arising**
> 4 **Business review**
> 5 **Targets**
> 6 **Promotions**
> 7 **Visits**
> 8 **Street food analysis**
> 9 **New product launch**
> 10 **Any other business**
> 11 **Date and time of next meeting**

1 Load up the outline agenda saved as **UNIT14-1.DOC** in Activity 1
2 Using the agenda headings, key in the minutes given on this and the following 2 pages, using styles as shown
3 Check the spelling and save
4 Print one copy on A4 or 11" continuous stationery

MINUTES

Minutes of a meeting of Midlands Sales Staff at Soar House, New Road, Leicester, on Wednesday, 12 March 19.., at 1000 hours.

Present

Michael Schaal (Chairman)	Chris Booth
Carol Breedon	Kelly Jay
Mike Oates	Judy Prior
Tina Salami	Anne Simpson
Nat Singh	Paul Ure
Jo Van Gyseghem	Brad West
Tam Wyatt	Mel Winters (Secretary)

1 Apologies
Apologies were received from Tod Crisp and Helen Danvers.

2 Minutes of last meeting
The minutes of the last meeting, which had been circulated, were confirmed as a true record and signed by the Chairman.

3 Matters arising
Paul Ure reported that all his attempts at retaining the key account with Macedon's Stores had proved abortive. The Chairman said that he would have a word with him on the subject after the meeting.

4 Business review
The Chairman presented charts and graphs showing the present position in the Midlands. The Company was 37% below target in the present financial year; the area 19% below. The Chairman was pleased to note that the area was performing significantly better than the national trends and was certain that a small surplus could be made at the year end in December. Sales of boxed chocolates and chocolate bars had fallen considerably and this would be one of the topics of discussion at the next meeting. He said that, overall, the picture was gloomy and great efforts would have to be made by the entire Midlands sales force in order to reverse the trend. In response to questions, he acknowledged that poor trade was a reflection of the current economic climate.

5 Targets
Tam Wyatt circulated copies of the February sales results. The Chairman congratulated Tina Salami on achieving top sales and said that she had become a valuable team member.

6 Promotions

Kelly Jay presented the promotions planned in April. These were aimed at the health bar market and included 2 nut and fruit bar promotions of 'Nutbic'- 'Buy five - get one free'.

It was intended to consolidate the street food promotions by providing a flash pack reducing 'Slick' bars from 24p each to 19p. Due to the flagging sales of the family chocolate bar, there would be a promotion on the Golden bar range offering a 10p money-back coupon on next purchase.

Sales promotional materials, samples and dump bins were provided for sales people to collect at the end of the meeting.

7 Visits

Individual reports on sales visits were presented by the 4 Sales Managers:

> Jo Van Gyseghem
> Judy Prior
> Anne Simpson
> Brad West

The Chairman congratulated the Managers on the enthusiasm and dedication of themselves and their staff and urged them on to even greater efforts.

8 Street food analysis

Market research reports showed that the chocolate bar which could be eaten in the street was still popular although sales overall were affected by the current diet trend. Low calorie foods were selling well and new products would be aimed at that market; namely diet street food.

9 New product launch

The Chairman announced that the new chocolate bar 'Panther' would be launched in May. Technical problems had caused the delay. Tasting samples in all 4 flavours were circulated and bulk supplies would be available after the meeting. Sales people should use promotional and merchandising materials distributed at the December conference. The publicity had been widespread and the product should do well.

10 Any other business

10.1 **Company Cars** Nat Singh asked if the Chairman knew of any change in policy on company cars. The Chairman replied that he had heard various rumours circulating but these were without foundation and there was no change in policy.

10.2 **Redundancies** Carol Breedon asked if there was any truth in the rumour regarding redundancies in the firm as a whole. The Chairman said that some cut backs would be necessary but that it was hoped to achieve these by natural wastage; no redundancies were planned at this time.

10.3 **Charities** Chris Booth suggested that a promotion should be launched whereby a small percentage was donated to charity. The Chairman asked the Secretary to place this on the agenda for the next meeting.

11 Date and time of next meeting

The next meeting would be held at the Nottingham offices at 1000 hours, on Wednesday, 8 April.

1 Load up the minutes, saved as **UNIT14-1.DOC** in Activity 2. Set up a one line footer in 8 point for every page of the document as follows
Left hand margin - *British Chocolates plc*
2 Put in a page number at the bottom right hand margin
3 Set up a one line header in 8 point for every page as follows
Centred - *Minutes - Midland Sales Staff*;   Right justified - *12 March 19xx*
4 Preview to make sure that the header and footer have been correctly set up and are displayed on each page

14.3 Editing a header or footer

Follow the same procedure as for setting up a header or footer and edit the text in the header or footer pane.

14.4 Ending pages

Page ends are generated automatically by Word for Windows when you have entered the number of lines which fill the current page size. You may want to end a page sooner than this, to keep text together with its heading, for example.

1 Move the insertion point to where the page is to end, preferably at the left margin.

2 Select **Break** from the **Insert** menu to display the **Break** dialog box.

3 Click on the **Page Break** radio button, if necessary and select **OK**. The next page will be displayed.

Break

Insert:
● Page Break
○ Column Break

OK
Cancel

Section Break
○ Next Page   ○ Even Page
○ Continuous   ○ Odd Page

14.5 Printing selected pages

1 Open the file which is to be printed, to display it on screen.

2 Select **Print** from the **File** menu and key in the starting and ending pages for printing in the dialog box.

3 The chosen pages will be printed.

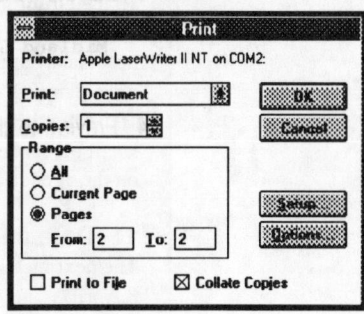

Print

Printer: Apple LaserWriter II NT on COM2:

Print: Document

Copies: 1

OK
Cancel

Range
○ All
○ Current Page
● Pages
From: 2   To: 2

Setup
Options

☐ Print to File   ☒ Collate Copies

1 Load up the minutes saved as **UNIT14-1.DOC**

2 Add blank lines after each heading and indent the main text under each heading, as shown below

---

1 Apologies

Apologies were received from Tod Crisp and Helen Danvers.

2 Minutes of last meeting

The minutes of the last meeting, which had been circulated, were confirmed as a true record and signed by the Chairman.

3 Matters arising

Paul Ure reported that all his attempts at retaining the key account with Macedon's Stores had proved abortive. The Chairman said that he would have a word with him on the subject after the meeting.

4 Business review

The Chairman presented charts and graphs showing the present position in the Midlands. The Company was 37% below target in the present financial year; the area 19% below. The Chairman was pleased to note that the Area was performing significantly better than the national trends and was certain that a small surplus could be made at the year end in December. Sales of boxed chocolates and chocolate bars had fallen considerably and this would be one of the topics of discussion at the next meeting. He said that, overall, the picture was gloomy and great efforts would have to be made by the entire Midlands sales force in order to reverse the trend. In response to questions, he acknowledged that poor trade was a reflection of the current economic climate.

5 Targets

Tam Wyatt circulated copies of the February sales results. The Chairman congratulated Tina Salami on achieving top sales and said that she had become a valuable team member.

---

3 Edit the header to be displayed as shown below and in the sample document on page 84

Midland Sales Staff   Wed 12 March

4 Preview to check the heading and save, before continuing with the editing

Activity 4

1 Set an additional tab at .75" (2 cm), before section 10 of the minutes, and indent the sub-sections to the second tab, as shown

---

10 Any other business

10.1 Company Cars Nat Singh asked if the Chairman knew of any change in policy on company cars. The Chairman replied that he had heard various rumours circulating but these were without foundation and there was no change in policy.

10.2 Redundancies Carol Breedon asked if there was any truth in the rumour regarding redundancies in the firm as a whole. The Chairman said that some cut backs would be necessary but that it was hoped to achieve these by natural wastage; no redundancies were planned at this time.

10.3 Charities Chris Booth suggested that a promotion should be launched whereby a small percentage was donated to charity. The Chairman asked the Secretary to place this on the agenda for the next meeting.

---

2 Move through the whole document, putting in page breaks to keep complete items with their heading, i e page breaks should be immediately *before* a heading
3 Print the second page, to check the layout and the header and footer and save again

Important You may sometimes want to fit a multi-page document onto fewer pages, for example to make photocopying cheaper. The easiest way to do this is to reduce the size of the main text, particularly if you are using styles. All you have to do is to edit your Normal style; the document will be re-formatted automatically to fit the new size.

Activity 5

1 Load up the minutes again
2 Take out the page breaks you put in, as they will be inappropriate when the text size has been changed
3 Highlight any portion of text which has the style Body Text
4 Edit the Body Text style to use 8 point or 15 cpi, whichever is available on your printer
5 Preview the document, then insert a page break, if necessary
6 Save and print
7 Your document should look like the sample document shown on the next two pages

MINUTES

Minutes of a meeting of Midlands Sales Staff at Soar House, New Road, Leicester, on Wednesday, 12 March 19.xx at 1000 hours.

Present

Michael Schaal (Chairman)	Chris Booth
Carol Breedon	Kelly Jay
Mike Oates	Judy Prior
Tina Salami	Anne Simpson
Nat Singh	Paul Ure
Jo Van Gyseghem	Brad West
Tam Wyatt	Mel Winters (Secretary)

1 Apologies

Apologies were received from Tod Crisp and Helen Danvers.

2 Minutes of last meeting

The minutes of the last meeting, which had been circulated, were confirmed as a true record and signed by the Chairman.

3 Matters arising

Paul Ure reported that all his attempts at retaining the key account with Macedon's Stores had proved abortive. The Chairman said that he would have a word with him on the subject after the meeting.

4 Business review

The Chairman presented charts and graphs showing the present position in the Midlands. The Company was 37% below target in the present financial year; the area 19% below. The Chairman was pleased to note that the area was performing significantly better than the national trends and was certain that a small surplus could be made at the year end in December. Sales of boxed chocolates and chocolate bars had fallen considerably and this would be one of the topics of discussion at the next meeting. He said that, overall, the picture was gloomy and great efforts would have to be made by the entire Midlands sales force in order to reverse the trend. In response to questions, he acknowledged that poor trade was a reflection of the current economic climate.

5 Targets

Tam Wyatt circulated copies of the February sales results. The Chairman congratulated Tina Salami on achieving top sales and said that she had become a valuable team member.

6 Promotions

Kelly Jay presented the promotions planned in April. These were aimed at the health bar market and included 2 nut and fruit bar promotions of 'Nutbic'- 'Buy five - get one free'.

It was intended to consolidate the street food promotions by providing a flash pack reducing 'Slick' bars from 24p each to 19p. Due to the flagging sales of the family chocolate bar, there would be a promotion on the Golden bar range offering a 10p money-back coupon on next purchase.

Sales promotional materials, samples and dump bins were provided for sales people to collect at the end of the meeting.

British Chocolates plc

1

7 Visits

Individual reports on sales visits were presented by the 4 Sales Managers:

Jo Van Gyseghem
Judy Prior
Anne Simpson
Brad West

The Chairman congratulated the Managers on the enthusiasm and dedication of themselves and their staff and urged them on to even greater efforts.

8 Street food analysis

Market research reports showed that the chocolate bar which could be eaten in the street was still popular although sales overall were affected by the current diet trend. Low calorie foods were selling well and new products would be aimed at that market; namely diet street food.

9 New product launch

The Chairman announced that the new chocolate bar 'Panther' would be launched in May. Technical problems had caused the delay. Tasting samples in all 4 flavours were circulated and bulk supplies would be available after the meeting. Sales people to use promotional and merchandising materials distributed at the December conference. The publicity had been widespread and the product should do well.

10 Any other business

10.1 **Company Cars** Nat Singh asked if the Chairman knew of any change in policy on company cars. The Chairman replied that he had heard various rumours circulating but these were without foundation and there was no change in policy.

10.2 **Redundancies** Carol Breedon asked if there was any truth in the rumour regarding redundancies in the firm as a whole. The Chairman said that some cut backs would be necessary but that it was hoped to achieve these by natural wastage; no redundancies were planned at this time.

10.3 **Charities** Chris Booth suggested that a promotion should be launched whereby a small percentage was donated to charity. The Chairman asked the Secretary to place this on the agenda for the next meeting.

11 Date and time of next meeting

The next meeting would be held at the Nottingham offices at 1000 hours, on Wednesday, 8 April.

1 Any multi-page document

2 Books and articles

3 Reports (*see* Unit 17)

4 Newsletters (*see* Unit 21)

• *The text is printed across the perforation on continuous stationery.*

You did not set the top of page setting on your printer before you started. On many printers, there is a button which does this. Set top of page or re-load the paper, and print again.

• *Your document does not fit on the same number of pages as in the example.*

The spacing set for your printer is probably slightly different from the laser printer used to produce the sample. Reduce the size of your text still further, if this is possible, or use slightly smaller left and right margins.

• *Even though you have reset the top of the page on your printer, the pages do not fit on A4 single sheet paper; a few lines have to be printed on the next sheet.*

Your printer may be set to leave a margin before it starts to print. You may be able to set the **printer's** top margin to be very small - you will need to refer to the manual.

• *When using single sheets, the printer stops before the bottom of the page is printed and asks for another sheet.*

The printer's paper sensor reports that there is no paper before the bottom of the page, as it is positioned on the bottom of the roller. Set a larger bottom margin on your page layout to deal with this. You may need to experiment to get this right.

• *You cannot print selected pages only.*

You used the **Print** button from the toolbar, rather than selecting **Print** from the **File** menu. The button only allows you to print **all** pages.

• *You could not see your header or footer on screen to check it.*

You changed to **Normal** view to set up your header/footer. In this view, you have the special header and footer panes available and can use the buttons for time, date and page number. To see the header and footer with your text, select **Page Layout** from the **View** menu and use the scroll bars to move to the top and bottom of the page.

Unit 15

Mailmerge

Overview There are many circumstances in which you may want to produce personalised letters to be sent to a large number of individuals or firms. Word for Windows can help you to do this automatically.

Existing skills
- Business letter layout - Unit 6
- Automatic date - Unit 6
- Tabs - Unit 7

New skills
- Setting up a file for variable details
- Setting up a letter for mailmerge
- Inserting variable details to produce a personalised letter

Important You may need to split up your data into a number of separate items, in order to use it in a number of different ways, eg postcodes often need to be separate, as do the separate parts of names.

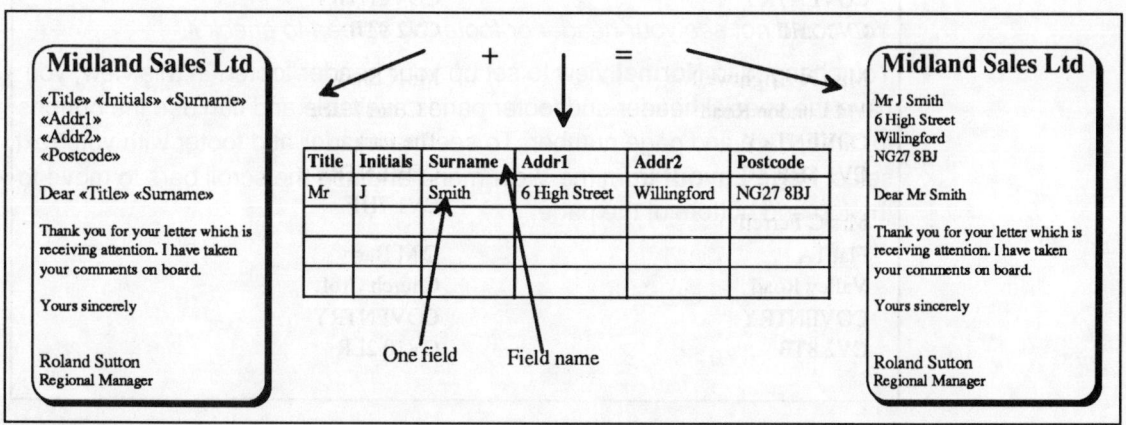

15.1 Setting up a data file

To merge data, you use a special type of file which contains only the variable information. The data in this file is made up of records, each containing a set of information about one person, split into fields. It is best to set this up before creating the main file which is to have the variables added to it. One data file is, in any case, likely to be used with a number of main files.

1 Open a new file and select **Print Merge** from the **File** menu.

2 Click the **Attach Data File** button in the dialog box.

3 Click the **Create Data File** button in the next dialog box.

4 Type in the name of each field in turn in the **Field Name** box and press **Return**.

5 Click **OK** and type in a file name for the data.

6 The table set up for the data in the file will be displayed with the headings already set. Key in the data, using the Tab key to move between fields and records. Leave blank any field which does not have an entry for a particular individual.

7 Save the file to disk.

Activity 1

1 Set up a new data file called **CUSTOMER.DOC**, with fields Title, Initials, Surname, Addr1, Addr2, Addr3, Postcode

2 Enter the following customer details into it, being sure to split up the elements of the names, so that they can be used in the address and after *Dear*

3 Save the file and print a copy for reference

Mr C Able	Mr I Rachins
56 Mere Green	98 Templeton Road
COVENTRY	COVENTRY
CV1 2HF	CV2 9TB
Miss N Brightwell	Mr N Shaw
114 London Road	3 Court Place
COVENTRY	The Park
CV1 5HF	COVENTRY
	CV1 7HF
Mrs C Ferrell	
Flat 1A	C M Barry
Valley Road	Church Croft
COVENTRY	COVENTRY
CV2 8TB	CV10 2LR

15.2 Setting up the main file

1 Open a new file and select **Print Merge** from the **File** menu.

2 Click the **Attach Data File** button in the dialog box and select the data file which you are going to use.

3 Key in the document as normal, but whenever you reach a point where an item of variable data is required, click on the **Insert Merge Field** button in the special **Print Merge** bar.

4 Double click on the field you require. It will be inserted in your document.

5 Save the file to disk for later use.

Activity 2

1 Key in the following letter, generating the date automatically
2 Insert the fields from the data file **CUSTOMER.DOC** set up in Activity 1, as shown
3 Proofread on screen and save to disk as **LETTER.DOC**
4 Print a reference copy

Today's date

«Title» «Initials» «Surname»
«Addr1»
«Addr2»
«Addr3»
«Postcode»

Dear «Title» «Surname»

I hope that you have enjoyed many miles of trouble free motoring since you bought your car from Arthur Swan of Coventry.

Although at the time of purchase you did not take up the option of the extended warranty available for second and third year parts and labour cover, it is not too late.

If you have reconsidered and would now like to take advantage of the offer which could bring you another 2 years' motoring with the consequent peace of mind, please contact Richard Lister on 0203 566321.

Yours sincerely

RICHARD LISTER
Business Manager

Mailmerge **89**

15.3 Merging two files

Merging files uses a great deal of memory, so it is very important to make sure that you have no other applications running at the same time.

1 Close all files except the two files you are merging, to release memory.

2 Make the main file the active one, ie the one containing the fields into which data is to be read.

3 Select **Print Merge** from the **File** menu and then **Merge**. If you want to display each copy on screen before printing, for a visual check, then click on **Record Selection**.

4 Check the printer is ready and click **OK**.

Activity 3

1 Use the files **LETTER.DOC** and **CUSTOMER.DOC** to produce the 6 letters required

2 Check that the first one comes out like the specimen shown below

---

Today's date

Mr C Able
56 Mere Green
COVENTRY
CV1 2HF

Dear Mr Able

I hope that you have enjoyed many miles of trouble free motoring since you bought your car from Arthur Swan of Coventry.

Although at the time of purchase you did not take up the option of the extended warranty available for second and third year parts and labour cover, it is not too late.

If you have reconsidered and would now like to take advantage of the offer which could bring you another 2 years' motoring with the consequent peace of mind, please contact Richard Lister on 0203 566321.

Yours sincerely

RICHARD LISTER
Business Manager

---

1 Create a new main file with the filename **LETTER2.DOC**, inserting the necessary fields where required
2 Use this new file with the file **CUSTOMER.DOC** to produce letters
3 Print the merged letters. The first one should look like the sample

---

Today's date

Mr C Able
56 Mere Green
COVENTRY
CV1 2HF

Dear Mr Able

Grand Opening

You may have noticed from local advertisements that we have moved our premises to the above address. As a privileged customer we would like to invite you to our Grand Opening on Saturday, 8 August, when you will be given a tour of our showrooms and works, followed by an entertainment and refreshments.

We think that you will find our servicing arrangements more than satisfactory at the new premises as we now provide free transport for you whilst your car is being serviced or, if more convenient, a car is loaned to you.

We shall look forward to seeing you on 8 August.

Yours sincerely

RICHARD LISTER
Business Manager

---

1 Producing automatic labels (*see* Unit 16)

2 Producing personalised invitations

3 Any mailshot

• *There are no spaces between the separate parts of the names in the letter, either in the name and address section, or after Dear.*

You did not press the space bar between fields to give the required spacing in the main file. Open the main file, if necessary, and put in the extra spaces.

• *One of your letters has jumbled fields, eg Miss 114 London Road.*

You have missed out a field in this record in your data file, making all the rest move up to fill the space. Check your data file to make sure that all 7 fields are present in every record, even when one is blank.

• *You are using single sheets of paper and only one letter has been printed.*

The printer may be waiting for another sheet of paper, so you will need to load one.

• *When you click on **Record Selection** the message 'Print Interrupt' is displayed.*

Click on the **Retry** box to try printing again. If this does not work, check that your printer is switched on, connected, on-line and has paper loaded.

Unit 16

Labels and envelopes

Once you have a file of names and addresses, you can use them for several purposes, including producing labels automatically for the letters you have mailmerged, and for printing directly on to envelopes. In Word for Windows, producing labels is set up as a macro.

Existing skills
- Changing page size - Unit 12
- Setting up a file for mailmerge - Unit 15
- Setting up a data file - Unit 15

New skills
- To produce labels automatically
- To print directly to envelopes

Important If your sheet or continuous label stationery is not a standard American size, then you cannot just use the template file and macro which have been set up, Instead, you can send your merged label file to disk and then print it out later, having made some adjustments by hand.

If you are using single sheet labels on a laser printer, then remember that most lasers cannot print closer than 0.5" to each edge. Similarly, if you are loading single sheets into a matrix or inkjet printer by hand, without a single sheet feeder, you will not be able to print very close to the top or bottom of the page.

It is always worth trying out label printing on blank paper before loading labels. They are relatively expensive!

16.1 Printing labels

A special template is provided with Word for Windows which you can use to produce mailing labels.

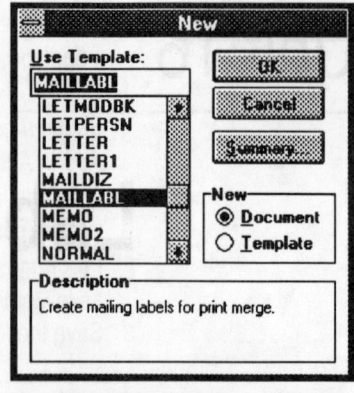

1 Set up a data file for your label data (*see* Unit 15) and save it to disk.

2 Select **New** from the **File** menu and select the template file **MAILLABL.DOT**, to use the label template and macro provided.

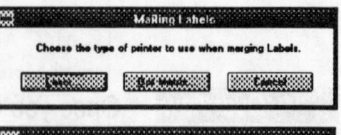

3 Select the type of printer you are going to use from the **Mailing Labels** dialog box.

4 Select the label size you want to use from the **Label Sizes** dialog box. You may have to choose the nearest one, as these are all special American sizes.

5 Select **Multiple labels** from the box displayed, followed by your data file.

6 The **Layout Mailing Labels** dialog box will be displayed. Using this, you can select the fields you need for your label and build up the exact layout.

7 Click on **Done** and then save your document. Then choose **Print Merge** from the **File** menu, followed by **Merge**.

16.2 Adding records to a data file

1 Load up your data file. The **Record Management Tools** command will be added to the **Tools** menu.

2 Select this command, and then select **Add New Record**. Add any additional records as required.

1 If you have completed Unit 15, and so have the file **CUSTOMER.DOC** saved on disk, open it and add the 6 additional names and addresses to it
   or
   Set up a new data file called **CUSTOMER.DOC**, with fields Title, Initials, Surname, Addr1, Addr2, Addr3, Postcode (*see* Unit 15)
   Enter the following customer details into it, being sure to split up the elements of the names into the correct fields

2 Proofread the file on screen, particularly the postcodes. Spell checking is not appropriate, as few of the words used would be in the dictionary

3 Save the file and print a copy for reference

Mr C Able
56 Mere Green
COVENTRY
CV1 2HF

Miss N Brightwell
114 London Road
COVENTRY
CV1 5HF

Mrs C Ferrell
Flat 1A
Valley Road
COVENTRY
CV2 8TB

Mr I Rachins
98 Templeton Road
COVENTRY
CV2 9TB

Mr N Shaw
3 Court Place
The Park
COVENTRY
CV1 7HF

Mr C M Barry
Church Croft
COVENTRY
CV10 2LR

Mr J Adcock
75 Springfield Road
COVENTRY
CV1 5HP

Mr K Douglas
103 Stafford Way
COVENTRY
CV22 4JN

Mr S Patel
49 Tandy Road
COVENTRY
CV2 7TB

Miss R Koscina
4 The Grove
COVENTRY
CV3 2BN

Ms C Viharo
43 Hunter's Cross
Bell Green
COVENTRY
CV1 9FH

A B Smith
23 Rectory Road
The Park
COVENTRY
CV1 8XJ

Activity 2

1 Key in the following text, which consists entirely of field names from the data file **CUSTOMER.DOC**, separated with spaces and Returns

«Title» «Initials» «Surname»
«Addr1»
«Addr2»
«Addr3»
«Postcode»

2 Save as the file **LABEL.DOC**
3 Print merge the labels by merging the files **LABEL.DOC** and **CUSTOMER.DOC**
4 Preview to check the display and print on plain paper for test purposes

Mr C Able 56 Mere Green COVENTRY CV1 2HF	Miss N Brightwell 114 London Road COVENTRY CV1 5HF
Mrs C Ferrell Flat 1A Valley Road COVENTRY CV2 8TB	Mr I Rachins 98 Templeton Road COVENTRY CV2 9TB
Mr N Shaw 3 Court Place The Park COVENTRY CV1 7HF	Mr C M Barry Church Croft COVENTRY CV10 2LR
Mr J Adcock 75 Springfield Road COVENTRY CV1 5HP	Mr K Douglas 103 Stafford Way COVENTRY CV22 4JN
Mr S Patel 49 Tandy Road COVENTRY CV2 7TB	Miss R Koscina 4 The Grove COVENTRY CV3 2BN
Ms C Viharo 43 Hunter's Cross Bell Green COVENTRY CV1 9FH	A B Smith 23 Rectory Road The Park COVENTRY CV1 8XJ

16.3 Using envelopes

Word for Windows has a specially set up system for printing envelopes, which makes use of the facilities offered by your printer.

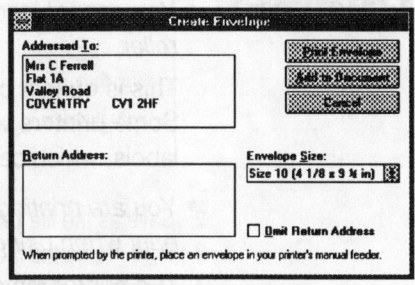

1 Key in the address you want on the envelope and highlight it with the mouse.

2 Select the **Envelope** button from the toolbar to display the Create Envelope dialog box.

3 If you do not want a return address (little used in UK), check this box.

4 Click on the arrow beside the envelope size box to display the options available and choose the closest size to the envelopes you want to use.

5 If you have a special envelope feeder on your printer, then use it. Otherwise, feed the envelope manually into the printer; you may have to remove the tractor feed on a matrix or inkjet printer.

6 Select **Print Envelope** and follow any special screen instructions given for your printer *(as on the screen shown above)*.

Activity 3

1 Key in the four names and addresses given and highlight each in turn
2 Select the envelope button to display the Create Envelope dialog box.
3 Choose envelope size C6 and no return address
4 Print the first envelope on to plain paper for practice
5 Create each of the other three envelopes in the same way

Mr S Patel
49 Tandy Road
COVENTRY
CV2 7TB

Miss R Koscina
4 The Grove
COVENTRY
CV3 2BN

Ms C Viharo
43 Hunter's Cross
Bell Green
COVENTRY
CV1 9FH

A B Smith
23 Rectory Road
The Park
COVENTRY
CV1 8XJ

A B Smith
23 Rectory Road
The Park
COVENTRY
CV1 8XJ

1 Multiple tickets

2 Badges

• *You cannot load envelopes into your printer, or they get stuck round the roller.*

This is quite a common problem, which may not have a direct solution. Some printers will not reliably load envelopes. Your best strategy is to use labels, which can then be stuck onto the envelopes.

• *You are printing on a laser printer which just puts on a light and does not print when using envelope printing.*

The printer may be waiting for you to feed an envelope manually, as it has no special envelope feeder. There should be a message at the bottom of the dialog box, if your printer has a standard Windows printer driver. Try loading a piece of paper by hand to test printing.

• *When you choose the MAILLABL.DOT template file with the **New** command, no dialog boxes are displayed for you to use for your labels, as shown in the instructions.*

You have chosen the **New** button from the toolbar, rather than selecting **New** from the **File** menu. The template and label macro are only invoked from the menu selection. Follow the procedure given again, using the menu selection.

• *You have typed all lower case characters by mistake, instead of upper case.*

You have pressed the Caps Lock key which gives lower case letters with the Shift key. Highlight the text which is lower case and select **Character** from the **Format** menu to display the **Character** dialog box. Click on the **All Caps** box to turn your text to capital letters.

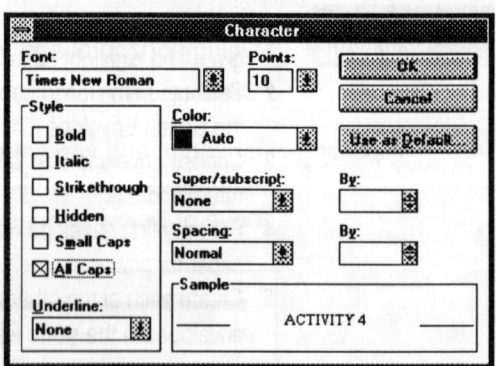

Unit 17

Reports

Overview Reports look most professional when they have sections headed in a 'hierarchical' and consistent way. Outlining in Word for Windows allows you to carry out this process automatically, using any numbering scheme you specify, eg 1.1, 1.2, 1.2.1 or 1 a), 1 b), etc, and to organise your text in a hierarchical way.

Existing skills
- Checking spelling - Unit 2
- Inserting the date automatically - Unit 6
- Changing fonts- Unit 11

New skills
- Using horizontal and vertical ruling lines
- Creating and using outlines

Important Horizontal and vertical ruling lines are used to give emphasis to text used in headings. Horizontal lines usually start at a margin and are placed directly above or below text, as in the examples below.

Two lines between margins

Lines as long as the text

One line below

Vertical lines are most commonly put in margins to show revisions, or as column markers.

17.1 Adding ruling lines to text

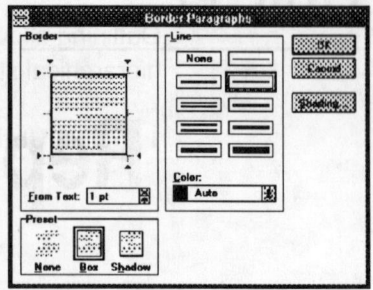

1 Highlight the text to which the ruling line, or border, is to be added.

2 Select **Border** from the **Format** menu to display the **Border Paragraphs** dialog box.

3 Select the preset border format **None** from the bottom of the box, and then choose a line above and/or below the text by clicking on the diagram.

4 Choose the width of line you want from the Line boxes, then choose any other lines you want and their width.

5 When you have chosen all the lines you want, click on **OK**.

17.2 Matching ruling lines to text length

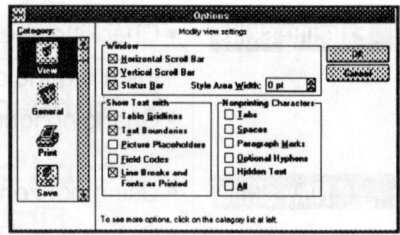

1 Select **Options** from the **Tools** menu and select **Line Breaks And Fonts As Printed**.

2 Highlight the text which already has a ruling line between the margins.

3 Drag the right margin and indent markers on the ruler to change the length of the ruling line.

<table>
<tr><td>**Activity 1**</td><td>

1 Clear the screen, if necessary

2 Select A4 paper size, if necessary, with 1" margins all round

3 Enter the title **Report**, right justified, emboldened and in 18 point

4 Create two ruling lines which look like the ones shown in the sample below, i.e. the line above about 8 times as thick as the one below

5 Preview to check the display. Make any changes you need, including moving the second line slightly to take account of the exact size of text for your printer, using the **From Text** option in the dialog box

6 Save the heading as file **UNIT17-1.DOC** and print the heading, then check your output and make any changes you think necessary

</td></tr>
</table>

Report

17.3 Creating an outline

Outlining allows you to enter text in any order and then organise it into a hierarchical structure. This lets you draft text in note form and then expand it.

1 Select **Outline** from the **View** menu to display the Outline ribbon.

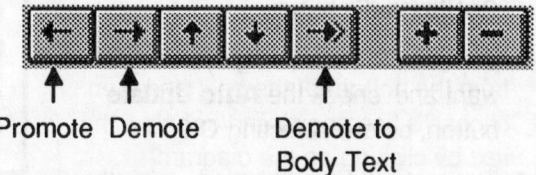

Promote Demote   Demote to
Body Text

2 Type a heading, followed by pressing **Return**.

3 Key in the next heading.

4 When you want to put in a heading at the next level down (or up), select the **Demote** (or **Promote**) button from the ribbon and key the text.

5 At each level, the text will be indented a further 0.5".

6 Any piece of text can be promoted or demoted by highlighting the text and then selecting **Demote** or **Promote**.

First heading

Second heading

First sub-heading

Second sub-heading

This is body text for entries of information under a heading.

Third heading

First sub-heading

First sub-section

Second sub-section

This is body text for entries of information under a heading.

17.4 Specifying outline numbering style

1 Highlight the complete piece of text to which you want to apply numbering.

2 Select **Bullets and Numbering** from the **Tools** menu and click on the **Outline** radio button.

3 Choose the numbering system you want and check the **Auto Update** button, before selecting **OK**.

4 The text will be numbered, using the levels you have chosen with your outlining.

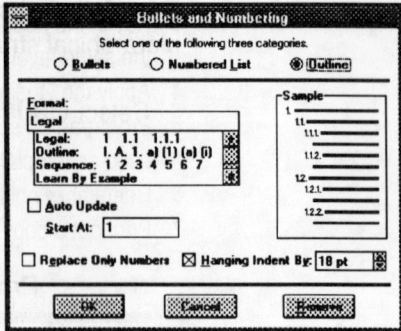

Activity 2

1 If you have already completed Unit 12, and so have file **AGENDA.DOC** stored on disk, then open it and delete the numbers and the blank lines between items
or
Key in the agenda below, omitting the item numbers

2 Specify legal numbering for outlines

3 Turn on OUTLINE mode and generate numbers for each item, with 2 spaces after it

4 Save and print one copy

A G E N D A

1 Apologies

2 Minutes of last meeting

3 Matters arising

4
5
6
7
8

9 Any other business

10 Date and time of next meeting

---

1 Open the file **UNIT17-1.DOC**, if it is not already on screen
2 Set page size to A4, if necessary
3 Key in the headings for the report template shown below in Outline view, making them all the same level.
4 Apply the Outline numbering style Legal to the headings
5 Proofread on screen and spell check. This is particularly important for files which are to be used as templates for other documents
6 Remember not to number the signature
7 Print out a copy for reference and save to disk as file **REPORT.DOC**

Report

To: Date:

1   **Subject:**

2   **Terms of Reference**

3   **Procedure**

4   **Findings**

5   **Conclusions**

6   **Recommendations**

Signature:
Designation:

1 If you have already completed Unit 14 and have **UNIT14-1.DOC** on disk, then open it
2 Choose legal numbering
3 Move through the minutes, removing the typed numbering and generating automatic numbers for each item
4 Preview, check the display and print, if desired

---

10 **Any other business**

10.1 **Company Cars** Nat Singh asked if the Chairman knew of any change in policy on company cars. The Chairman replied that he had heard various rumours circulating but these were without foundation and there was no change in policy.

10.2 **Redundancies** Carol Breedon asked if there was any truth in the rumour regarding redundancies in the firm as a whole. The Chairman said that some cut backs would be necessary but that it was hoped to achieve these by natural wastage; no redundancies were planned at this time.

---

1 Open the report template you prepared in Activity 3, saved on disk as **REPORT.DOC**, if it is not already on screen
2 Use the template to produce the report which is given below and on the next page. The sub-sections should be produced by typing in outline mode and demoting the text to the body text level
3 Generate numbering for the sections
4 Generate the date automatically
5 Remove any unwanted numbering in blank lines
6 Check the display, save and print

Report

To: The Managing Director   **Date:** Today's date

1 **Subject: FLEXITIME**

2 **Terms of Reference**

2.1 At your request, I undertook to ascertain whether the office staff would be prepared to change over to flexible working hours.

2.2 I also undertook to produce a report within four weeks.

---

3   Procedure

3.1   I initially circulated a questionnaire.

3.2   I followed this up with personal interviews, in order to establish the main body of opinion.

3.3   I made preliminary investigations into the equipment needed to run the scheme.

4   Findings

4.1   The results of the questionnaire and interviews were in favour of flexitime.

4.2   There were only two or three members of senior staff who would not welcome the change.

4.3   Most staff appreciated that they would be able to accommodate personal arrangements more easily and to accrue time sufficient to allow for the occasional long weekend.

5   Conclusions

5.1   I concluded that the change could be effected without opposition and with the minimum disruption of office procedures.

5.2   The advantages would include reducing the need for overtime and enabling staff to travel outside peak commuter hours.

5.3   The system should also eliminate bad timekeeping.

6   Recommendations

6.1   I recommend that the Company changes over to flexitime for office staff from the beginning of April.

6.2   An April start would allow sufficient time for the installation of a special time recorder and the issue of individual keys to all staff in the system.

Signature: Marie Bossicco
Designation: Personal Assistant

1 Vertical ruling lines between columns (*see* Unit 21)

2 Composing reports at the keyboard

3 Structuring any piece of work

Problem solving
- *One or both of your horizontal lines does not begin at the left margin and end at the right margin.*

  You set the horizontal position incorrectly.

- *Your horizontal lines are the same width, rather than thick above the text and thin below it.*

  You set an incorrect line width for one of them.

- *Your horizontal lines are the wrong way round, rather than thick above the text and thin below it.*

  You set an incorrect width for both lines.

- *The body of your report is overwritten by the second ruling line of the heading.*

  Your printer spacing leaves very little room above text. Insert a blank line before the first line of the report to leave a little more space for the ruling line.

- *You have no numbers in some lines where they are required.*

  No numbering is possible in lines which have no text in them. You will have to put in some text before the numbers will be filled in.

- *When you have selected double spacing, your highlighted text disappears.*

  You have pressed a key without first repositioning your cursor. When text is highlighted, typing deletes it and replaces it with the keyed characters. This is a very useful feature in editing, but a little worrying when it happens accidentally. Always reposition your cursor to remove highlighting when you have completed an operation, before continuing.

Unit 18

Legal documents

Overview Legal work should not be punctuated, as the language used should be sufficiently clear without the aid of such means of expression. The final copy of any legal document should be error free, so as to reduce the possibility of misinterpretation or fraud.

The clauses in legal documents are similar for each particular document, eg Conveyance, Agreement, Will, Trust Deed, and lend themselves to a WP library.

Existing skills
- Checking spelling - Unit 2
- Numbering paragraphs - Unit 5
- Setting tabs - Unit 7
- Changing fonts - Unit 11
- Splitting pages - Unit 14

New skills
- Double spacing

Important For legal work, you should spell check initially and then proofread carefully against your original.

18.1 Setting initial default font

1 Select **Character** from the **Format** menu to display the **Character** dialog box.

2 Select the downward arrow button beside the font box and then the font you want from the list displayed.

3 Click on **Use as Default** and then **OK**. All new text will now be in the new font.

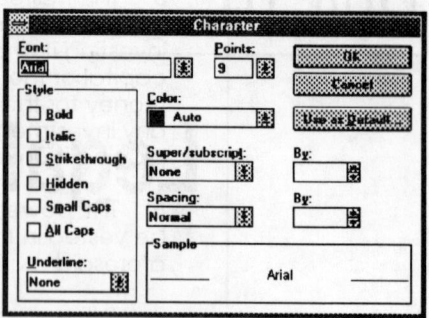

Activity 1

1 Clear the screen, if necessary, select a default font Helvetica 9 point (or Gothic, if you have it) and key in the following deed of trust

2 Spell check, proofread carefully and save on disk as **UNIT18-1.DOC**

DECLARATION OF THE TRUSTS OF THE EMMA SHAW MEMORIAL TRUST

THIS DECLARATION OF TRUST made on .... 19.. by Alan Holmes of 12 Kuster Road West Bridgford Nottingham and Marjory Elliott of 5 Wilmore Drive West Bridgford Nottingham and the Reverend Austen Williams of The Vicarage Church Road West Bridgford Nottingham (referred to herein as "the Trustees" which expression shall include the trustees for the time being of this deed)

WITNESSES as follows:

1 THERE IS established by this deed a charitable trust ("the Trust") to be known as The Emma Shaw Memorial Trust

2 THE objects of the Trust shall be to distribute and pay all money and other assets of the Trust (whether capital or income) to (whether capital or income) and for such charitable purposes and in such manner and in such proportions as the Trustees in their absolute discretion shall think fit AND in particular (though without prejudice to the generality of the foregoing) to and for the maintenance and support of persons connected with the Church of England in the Parish of St Peter's at West Bridgford who are engaged in a course of Christian study or who are training for the Ministry of the Church of England

3 THE initial money and assets of the Trust are as stated in the Schedule to this deed AND the Trustees may collect and receive money for the purposes of the Trust by donation or in such other lawful manner as they shall think fit

4 THE receipt of any person who shall be an object of or who shall be acting in any responsible capacity in respect of any charitable purpose shall be a good discharge to the Trustees for any payment or transfer of assets made for the relevant purpose

---

5   THE Trustees may for such period as is permitted by law in their absolute discretion accumulate all or any of the income of the Trust by investing it and shall hold such accumulations as an addition to the capital of the Trust AND the Trustees shall have power to invest any money for the time being not required for the purposes of the Trust in any investment authorised for the investment of trust money or by placing it on deposit at any bank or building society in Great Britain

6   THE power of appointing new or additional trustees of the Trust shall be vested in the Vicar for the time being of the Parish of St Peter's aforesaid

7   THE expression "charitable purposes" means purposes which are exclusively charitable according to the law for the time being of England and Wales

8   THE Trustees shall distribute the whole of the money and other assets held by them for the purposes of the Trust in accordance with clause 2 hereof on or before the expiration of one hundred years from the date hereof

9   IN WITNESS whereof the parties hereto have hereunto set their hands the day and year first before written

THE SCHEDULE

Three hundred and fifty thousand pounds invested in a Capital Reserve Account with the Cooperative Bank plc
Two hundred and five thousand pounds invested in a Gold Account with the Alliance and Leicester Building Society
Twenty five thousand pounds invested in a ninety day account with the Halifax Building Society
One thousand shares in British Telecom
Two thousand shares in British Gas

SIGNED AS A DEED by the said Alan Holmes   )
in the presence of   )

SIGNED AS A DEED by the said Marjory Elliott   )
in the presence of   )

SIGNED AS A DEED by the said Austen Williams   )
in the presence of   )

18.2 Setting double spacing

1 Select the paragraph which is to be double spaced (double click in the margin beside it).

2 Select **Paragraph** from the **Format** menu to display the **Paragraph** dialog box.

3 Select the downward arrow button beside the Line Spacing box and then **Double** from the list displayed.

4 Click on **OK**.

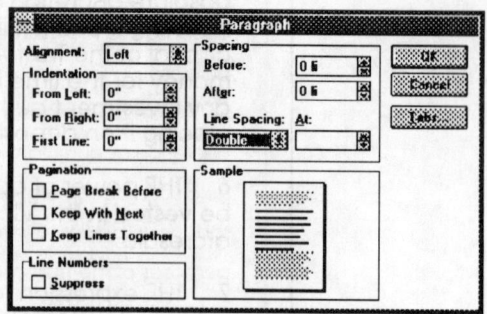

Activity 2

1 Retrieve the file **UNIT18-1.DOC**, if it is not already on screen

2 Delete the blank lines between paragraphs and set double spacing after the heading. Set single spacing again after the heading 'The Schedule'

3 Preview to check display, insert a page break in a suitable place, save and print

---

DECLARATION OF THE TRUSTS OF THE EMMA SHAW MEMORIAL TRUST

THIS DECLARATION OF TRUST made on .... 19.. by Alan Holmes of 12 Kuster Road West Bridgford Nottingham and Marjory Elliott of 5 Wilmore Drive West Bridgford Nottingham and the Reverend Austen Williams of The Vicarage Church Road West Bridgford Nottingham (referred to herein as "the Trustees" which expression shall include the trustees for the time being of this deed)

WITNESSES as follows:

1   THERE IS established by this deed a charitable trust ("the Trust") to be known as The Emma Shaw Memorial Trust

2   THE objects of the Trust shall be to distribute and pay all money and other assets of the Trust (whether capital or income) to (whether capital or income) and for such charitable purposes and in such manner and in such proportions as the Trustees in their absolute discretion shall think fit AND in particular (though without prejudice to the generality of the foregoing) to and for the maintenance and support of persons connected with the Church of England in the Parish of St Peter's at West Bridgford who are engaged in a course of Christian study or who are training for the Ministry of the Church of England

3   THE initial money and assets of the Trust are as stated in the Schedule to this deed AND the Trustees may collect and receive money for the purposes of the Trust by donation or in such other lawful manner as they shall think fit

---

4   THE receipt of any person who shall be an object of or who shall be acting in any responsible capacity in respect of any charitable purpose shall be a good discharge to the Trustees for any payment or transfer of assets made for the relevant purpose

5   THE Trustees may for such period as is permitted by law in their absolute discretion accumulate all or any of the income of the Trust by investing it and shall hold such accumulations as an addition to the capital of the Trust AND the Trustees shall have power to invest any money for the time being not required for the purposes of the Trust in any investment authorised for the investment of trust money or by placing it on deposit at any bank or building society in Great Britain

6   THE power of appointing new or additional trustees of the Trust shall be vested in the Vicar for the time being of the Parish of St Peter's aforesaid

7   THE expression "charitable purposes" means purposes which are exclusively charitable according to the law for the time being of England and Wales

8   THE Trustees shall distribute the whole of the money and other assets held by them for the purposes of the Trust in accordance with clause 2 hereof on or before the expiration of one hundred years from the date hereof

9   IN WITNESS whereof the parties hereto have hereunto set their hands the day and year first before written

THE SCHEDULE

Three hundred and fifty thousand pounds invested in a Capital Reserve Account with the Cooperative Bank plc
Two hundred and five thousand pounds invested in a Gold Account with the Alliance and Leicester Building Society
Twenty five thousand pounds invested in a ninety day account with the Halifax Building Society
One thousand shares in British Telecom
Two thousand shares in British Gas

SIGNED AS A DEED by the said   )
Alan Holmes in the presence   )
of   )

SIGNED AS A DEED by the said   )
Marjory Elliott in the   )
presence of   )

SIGNED AS A DEED by the said   )
Austen Williams in the   )
presence of   )

1 Variable line spacing is used when designing forms

2 Double or treble line spacing is used in drafts, literary work, legal documents or similar work

• *Not all the specified section of your final document is in double line spacing.* You had not highlighted all the section concerned when you selected double spacing. Highlight the paragraphs which are not double spaced again and select double spacing for them. Check the display.

• *Your brackets are not aligned before the signatures.* You did not use Tab to align them. Set up a tab stop at the appropriate place, if one does not already exist, and insert tabs before the brackets.

Unit 19

Literary work

Literary documents have a set of standard rules. Footnotes are used for explanation and headers and footers for chapters and the book title. Spelling is particularly important to give a good impression, and authors often use a Thesaurus to look up alternative words; to avoid using the same word several times, which is considered bad style.

Existing skills
- Checking spelling - Unit 2
- Indented paras - Unit 5
- Splitting pages - Unit 14
- Using headers and footers - Unit 14

New skills
- Using footnotes
- Using a Thesaurus

Important Footnotes are references or additional items of explanation inserted at the bottom of the appropriate page, with a small number, letter or character in the text for reference.

Footnotes are not necessarily displayed on the editing screen. They can be seen only in Page Layout view.

> Footnotes are references or additional items of explanation inserted at the bottom of the appropriate page, with a small number, letter or character in the text for reference.
> Footnotes[1] are references or additional items of explanation inserted at the bottom of the appropriate page, with a small number, letter or character in the text for reference.
> ------
> [1] This is the footnote

19.1 Creating a footnote

1 Position your cursor immediately after the word to which the footnote is to refer.

2 Select **Footnote** from the **Insert** menu to display the **Footnote** dialog box. Then click **OK** to accept the default numbering system and positioning.

3 Type in the footnote in the small pane opened at the bottom of the page beside the footnote number automatically displayed and then click on the page to go back to your text.

4 Carry out the same procedure for any further footnotes. They will be successively numbered.

19.2 Setting the footnote style

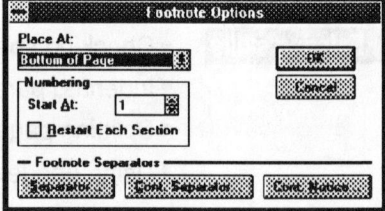

1 Select **Footnote** from the **Insert** menu and click on the **Custom Footnote Mark** box.

2 Key into the box the character you want, eg *.

3 Select the **Options** box to display the **Footnotes Option** dialog box.

4 Click on the **Place at** box and select the positioning you want from the list displayed.

5 Click on **OK** twice to return to your text.

Activity 1

1 Clear the screen, if necessary
2 Key in the Authors' Word Processing Rules, using the display given on page115.
3 Set up the footnotes shown on the sheet
4 Preview to check the display, save as **UNIT19-1DOC** and print

Word Processing for Authors

Word processing is an ideal author's tool, as alterations and redrafts are made easily and quickly. Literary work covers reports, articles, short stories, books or theses. There are a few rules to remember:

Stationery Usually one side of A4 is used.

Line Spacing Reports are usually single line spaced but manuscripts for books and stories should be double line spaced.

Margins Margins should not be less than 25 mm each side but if a binding margin is required the left margin should be 38 mm and the right 13 mm to 25 mm.[1] The top and bottom margins should be equal at 25 mm[2] except for chapter headings.

Pagination Use automatic pagination for numbering the pages. Ensure that single lines are not separated from the main text, leaving widows and orphans. Check that lists of items are not separated from one another. Use the 'widow/orphan protection' function to avoid mistakes.

Chapter heading The first page of a chapter is often in the form of a 'dropped head' which is when the chapter number is printed 51 mm to 76 mm from the top edge of the paper.

Layout The layout should be consistent throughout the work.

Footnotes Footnotes are usually printed at the foot of the page to which they refer. A number or symbol, such as asterisk, is shown in the text closed up to the referenced word. The footnote commences with the symbol and, after one space, the reference is given.

Spelling Check Make full use of the spelling check not only for misspelt words but also to pick up typos.

Thesaurus The Thesaurus is an invaluable tool in literary work.

Headers and Footers Headers and footers are useful in literary work. The header might be the title of the work and a footer, in addition to the page numbers, could give the author's name.

[1] If both sides of the paper are used, and the margins are unequal, then margins may be reversed on the continuation sheets.

[2] 1" in imperial measure.

19.3 Using the Thesaurus

A Thesaurus is a special sort of dictionary which gives alternative words (synonyms) with the same or a similar meaning. Word for Windows has a disk-based version which can be used when a word you have chosen does not seem to fit well, or has been used already in the same sentence or paragraph.

1 Highlight the word you wish to look up in the Thesaurus.

2 Select **Thesaurus** from the **Tools** menu to display the **Thesaurus** dialog box which shows the possible alternatives, with their meanings.

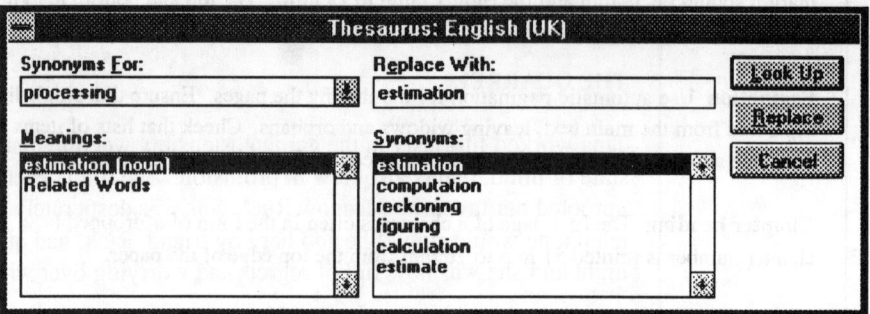

3 Select **Look Up** to further investigate the meaning of the word highlighted and its synonyms.

4 Select **Replace** to replace your word with the word which you have highlighted as the best alternative.

5 The word will be replaced in your text.

| Activity 2 |

1 Clear the screen, if necessary

2 If you have completed Unit 18 and so have **UNIT18-1.DOC** saved on disk, open it and find the word 'objects'
or
Key in the word 'objects'

3 Use the Thesaurus to choose an alternative for 'objects' which has the same meaning as in a legal document. *You will have to follow up its meaning*

Activity 3

1 Clear the screen and key in the following start of a romantic novel
2 Use the chapter number as a header and your own name as a footer
3 Use the spelling checker for corrections and then the Thesaurus to replace 'muttered' and 'worrying' with similar words
4 Remember that you will have to check that your choice of word fits, eg choosing 'laboured' to replace 'worked', rather than 'labour', which would not fit the sentence
5 Add the footnote which gives the Latin name of the plant
6 Use double line spacing and margins of 1.5" (37 mm), as wide spacing and margins are both essential requirements of manuscripts submitted for publication
7 Save as **UNIT19-1.DOC** and print

CHAPTER I

THE QUARREL

Tina worked furiously in the garden ostensibly weeding but, in her present state of mind, plants also flew in profusion. She didn't even notice when she uprooted her favourite Meadow Rue*. She was desperately hoping the telephone would ring. She and her boy friend, Rick, had quarrelled badly last night and she was now full of regrets and worrying over what they had said.

It was such a silly row and started over the meal. She had gone to a great deal of trouble to cook a special meal for their anniversary; it was one month since they had met. She had served melon and avocado cocktail followed by lemon chicken and she thought that her Charlotte Russe for dessert was a masterpiece. Rick had hardly eaten a thing and muttered something about a big lunch. She thought he'd spent too long at the pub before turning up and so, of course, her temper had risen. Before she realised it, they were both arguing and she said some things that she now regretted. Rick flung out of the flat and left her in tears amongst the debris of the meal.

She thought about the day that they had met. It was late on a Friday evening and she had gone down to her local supermarket to stock up for the week-end. She was just about to select a small chicken, when it was wrenched, almost from her hand, and she turned startled to find a tall, blonde and very handsome man had picked it up. As he met her indignant gaze, he realised what he had done and apologised profusely. He said 'May I buy you a drink to make amends for my bad manners?' Although Tina did not usually make casual dates, she found his steel grey eyes quite magnetic and found herself agreeing. Things had moved rapidly on from there.

* Thalictrum aquilegifolium

1 Explanatory notes in business documents

2 Choosing appropriate language for any composition work

• *A word you want to look up gives no alternatives.*

The word is not in the Thesaurus, so no alternatives are available. A disk based Thesaurus contains only a limited number of the most commonly used words, unlike the appropriate reference book.

• *The word you have chosen as an alternative from the Thesaurus does not seem to fit the sentence.*

You have chosen from the wrong list of alternatives for a word which has several different meanings. Change back to the original word, then use the Thesaurus again and choose from another list.

• *The word you have chosen as an alternative from the Thesaurus seems to change the meaning of the sentence.*

You may have chosen the antonym, which is the exact opposite in meaning for a word. Delete the word, key in the original word and choose again.

• *Your replacement word is not the one you thought you were choosing.*

You did not check that the word in the **Replace With** box was the one you wanted before clicking **OK**. Change back to the original word, then use the Thesaurus again and choose from the list again.

Unit 20

Scientific work

Overview When doing scientific work, you will need to use the special facilities in Word for Windows for producing equations.

Existing skills
- Enhancing text - Unit 3
- Using tables - Units 8 and 9

New skills
- Using subscript and superscript
- Using embedded applications
- Creating equations
- Creating graphs

Important The facilities provided in Word for Windows allow you to enter, display and edit an equation which forms an integral part of a document. The software does not allow you to make any calculations based on those equations.

The Equation Editor is one of the *embedded applications* which form an integral part of Word for Windows version 2; two others are Draw and Graph, which are used in Unit 21. All these applications work in the same way - they can be called up from Word and used to put information into frames.

Equation Editor	**Graph**	**Drawing**
$$y = \sqrt{\dfrac{x^2 - 4ab}{c^3}}$$		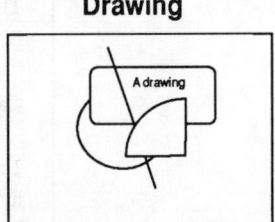

20.1 Using superscript

Superscript gives **raised** characters which should be about half the size of normal text in scientific/mathematical work, eg x^2.

1 Highlight the text to be enhanced.

2 Select **Character** from the **Format** menu to display the **Character** dialog box.

3 Click on the arrow beside the **Super/subscript** box and select **Superscript** from the list.

4 Choose a suitable point size for the superscripted text and click **OK**.

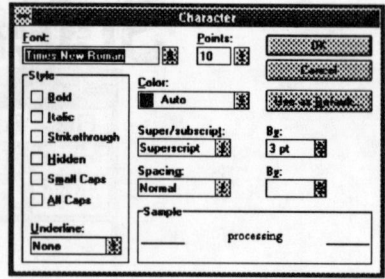

20.2 Using subscript

Subscript gives **lowered** characters which should be half the size of normal text in scientific/mathematical work eg X_0.

1 Highlight the text to be enhanced.

2 Select **Character** from the **Format** menu to display the **Character** dialog box.

3 Click on the arrow beside the **Super/subscript** box and select **Subscript** from the list.

4 Choose a suitable point size for the superscripted text and click **OK**.

Activity 1

1 Clear the screen, if necessary
2 Key in the following chemical explanation, following the display given
3 Check, save as **UNIT20-1.DOC** and print

Neutralising values

The equation for the reaction of calcium hydroxide (slaked lime) with hydrochloric acid is:

$$Ca(OH)_2(s) + 2HCl(aq) ===> CaCl_2(aq) + H_2O(l)$$

1 mol of calcium oxide neutralises the same amount of acid as 1 mol of calcium hydroxide.
The molar mass of calcium oxide = 56 g/mol
The molar mass of calcium hydroxide = 74 g/mol

20.3 Creating an equation

1 Position your cursor at the point in your text where the equation is to appear.

2 Select **Object** from the **Insert** menu, followed by **Equation** to load the built in **Equation Editor** application.

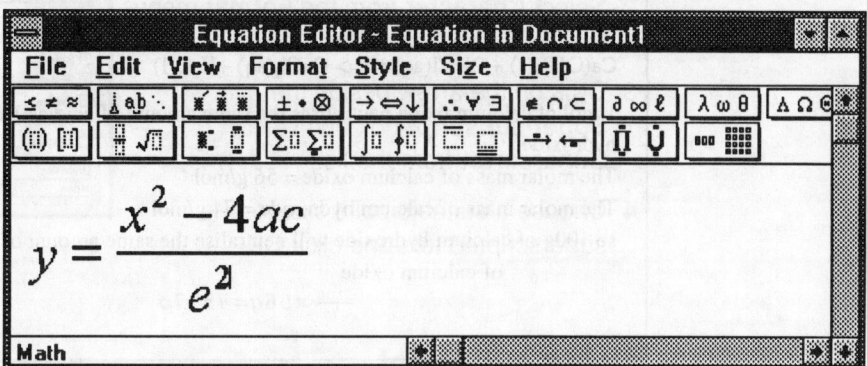

3 Key in your equation, using plus, minus, multiply * and divide /, selecting optional displays from the toolbar, by pointing with the mouse and holding down the left mouse button. You will probably use the 2 buttons shown on the left most often.

Fractions/
Radicals

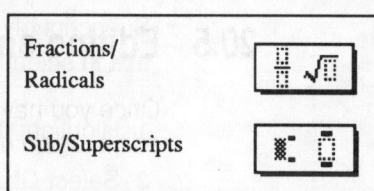

Sub/Superscripts

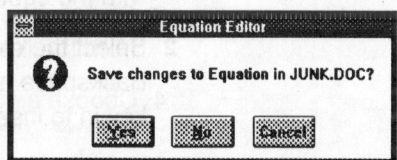

4 Select **Exit and Return to Filename** from the **File** menu to return to your text. A dialog box will be displayed.

5 Select **OK** to put the new equation into a frame in your document at the cursor position.

20.4 Positioning an equation

Once you have created an equation, you can move it about by clicking on it to select its surrounding frame. Then point anywhere inside the frame and drag it to the required position.

Activity 2

1 Open a new document
2 Use the Equation Editor to produce the formula shown in the demonstration screen above
3 Position it in the centre of the screen and key in a title for it
4 Save as **UNIT20-2.DOC** and print out a copy

1 Open the file **UNIT20-1.DOC**, if it is not already on screen
2 Add the equation to the file, as shown below
3 Save as and print

Neutralising values

The equation for the reaction of calcium hydroxide (slaked lime) with hydrochloric acid is:

$Ca(OH)_2(s) + 2HCl(aq) ===> CaCl_2(aq) + H_2O(l)$

1 mol of calcium oxide neutralises the same amount of acid as 1 mol of calcium hydroxide.

The molar mass of calcium oxide = 56 g/mol

The molar mass of calcium hydroxide = 74 g/mol

so 100g of calcium hydroxide will neutralise the same amount of acid as

of calcium oxide

$$\frac{100}{74} \times 56g = 75.7g$$

20.5 Editing an equation

Once you have inserted an equation into your document, you can very easily edit it, again using the Equation Editor.

1 Double click on the equation frame to open the Equation Editor application with the equation showing in the editing window.

2 Select the element in the equation which you want to change. Use the Backspace and Delete keys to delete items or select the tool you want and key in to insert new items.

1 Open the file **UNIT20-2.DOC**, if it is not already on screen
2 Edit the equation as shown below
3 Save the file and print out

$$y = \sqrt{\frac{(x^2 - 4xy + 2y)}{e^2}} + \frac{x}{y^3}$$

20.6 Creating a graph

You may find the ability to create and display graphs useful in mathematical and scientific work. A graph is treated as an object, just like an equation.

1 Select the **Graph** button from the toolbar or select **Object** from the **Insert** menu, followed by **Microsoft Graph** to load the built in **Graph** application.

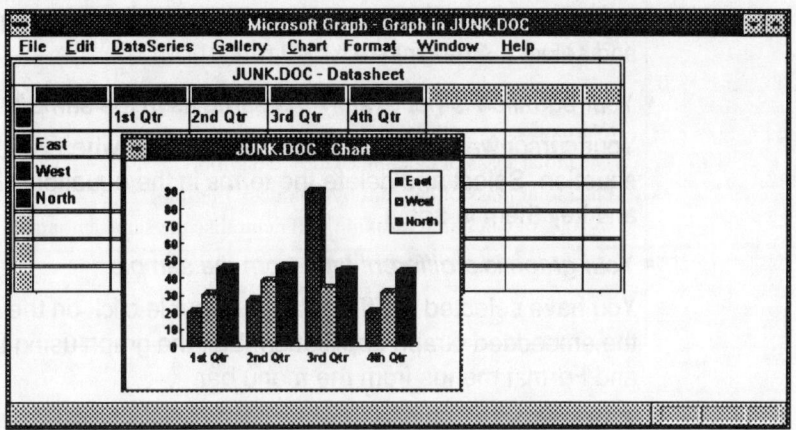

2 The default graph will be displayed, with its data.

3 Click on the Datasheet window or select **Datasheet** from the **Window** menu and key in the data you wish to graph. Alternatively, you can highlight a table of figures before you select the application and these will be used as the data for the graph.

4 Choose the style of graph you want from the **Gallery** menu and the titles etc, that you require from the **Chart** menu.

5 Select **Exit and Return to Filename** from the **File** menu to return to your text. A dialog box will be displayed.

6 Select **OK** to put the new graph into a frame in your document at the cursor position.

Activity 5

1 Set up the table given below and highlight the table and produce a Bar graph of its data
2 Position your graph at the right hand side of the table, as shown
3 Save the file containing the table and graph as **UNIT20-1.DOC** and print a copy

	Item 1	Item 2	Item 3
Day 1	120	96	151
Day 2	143	100	139
Day 3	160	115	119

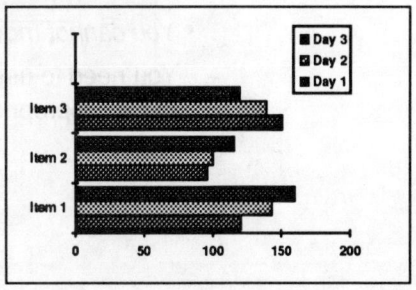

Further uses   1 Educational work

2 Mathematical work

Problem solving   • *Your subscripted and/or superscripted letters are the same size as ordinary text.*

You did not choose a smaller point size for the text. Highlight the text again and select a smaller size.

• *Your equation is not exactly the same as in the sample.*

Your cursor was probably in the wrong place when you keyed in part of the equation. Select and delete the terms in the equation which are incorrect and key them in again.

• *Your graph is a different type from the sample.*

You have selected a different type. Double click on the graph frame to load the embedded Graph application. Edit the graph using the Gallery, Chart and Format menus from the menu bar.

• *Your graph will not move to the position you want.*

The frame is moving with the text to keep in the same cursor position relative to your text when you created it. Select the frame and select **Frame** from the **Format** menu to display the **Frame** dialog box. If the **Move with Text** radio button is checked, then click on it to remove the check. Click on **OK**. You should then be able to reposition the frame as you choose.

• *Several more characters than you intended are superscripted/subscripted.*

You have continued typing with superscript or subscript selected. Select the menu again to switch off the enhancement.

• *You cannot find + - or = in the menus to put into your equations.*

These operators are not in menus; they must be keyed in normally in the appropriate positions. Double click on the equation frame and edit your equation to include the operators.

• *You cannot move around the datasheet to enter data.*

You need to use the mouse to move to each cell in the datasheet, clicking in the appropropriate cell.

Unit 21

Newsletters

Overview With Word for Windows and a suitable printer, you can produce a newsletter of a quality good enough for internal circulation. You can use quite complicated display, with unusual fonts, almost reaching the power of a DeskTop Publishing package.

Existing skills
- Changing text size - Unit 4
- Using styles - Unit 13
- Ruling lines - Unit 17

New skills
- Using multiple columns
- Creating drawings

Important Newspaper-style columns allow text to flow from the bottom of one column to the top of the next, as in a newspaper. Multiple columns with side-by-side information in them are best produced using a multi-line table (*see* Unit 9).

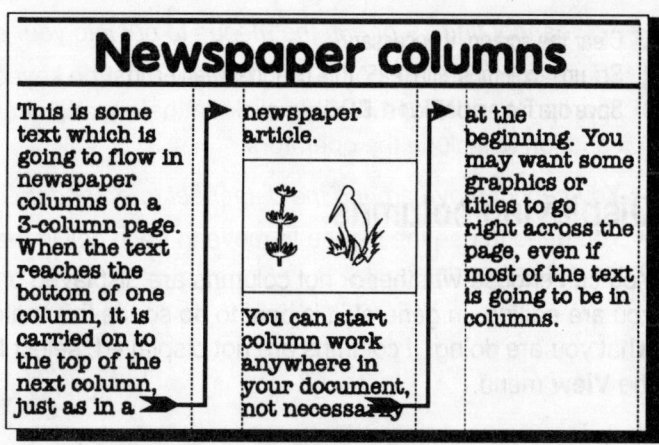

Newspaper columns

This is some text which is going to flow in newspaper columns on a 3-column page. When the text reaches the bottom of one column, it is carried on to the top of the next column, just as in a

newspaper article.

You can start column work anywhere in your document, not necessarily

at the beginning. You may want some graphics or titles to go right across the page, even if most of the text is going to be in columns.

21.1 Setting multiple columns

Using Word for Windows you can have a very large number of columns, but you will rarely want more than 3 or 4, unless you are using very small text.

1 Position the cursor at the point in your text where multiple columns are to begin.

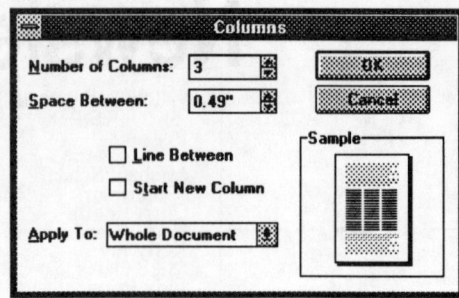

2 Select **Columns** from the **Format** menu to display the **Columns** dialog box.

3 Click on the up arrow beside the **Number of Columns** box until the number of columns you require is displayed. A sample of how the page will look is shown.

4 Select the **Space Between** box and type in the width you want. This is called the gutter.

5 Select the extent in your document to which the columns are to apply, ie Whole Document or This Point Forward. Click **OK** to return to your text.

21.2 Clearing multiple columns

1 Move the cursor to the point where multiple columns are to end.

2 Select **Columns** from the **Format** menu to display the **Columns** dialog box.

3 Set **Number of Columns** to 1 and click **OK**.

Activity 1

1 Clear the screen, if necessary
2 Set up 4 columns with 0.25" (0.6 cm) between each
3 Save the file as **UNIT21-1.DOC**

21.3 Displaying columns

You can choose whether or not columns are displayed on the screen while you are editing. In general, it is best to do so, as this makes it easier to see what you are doing. If columns are not displayed, select **Page Layout** from the **View** menu.

1 Open the file **UNIT21-1.DOC**, if it is not already on screen
2 If you have completed Unit 14, retrieve the minutes saved as **UNIT14-1.DOC** into this file. Alternatively, you can use the file **UNIT18-1.DOC**, the trust deed saved in Unit 18
3 Move the cursor to the first line after the heading and set up 4 columns. The top of your page should look like the sample shown below, although the columns may split differently
4 Save and print

Minutes of a meeting of Midlands Sales Staff at Soar House, New Road, Leicester, on Wednesday, 12 March 19.., at 1000 hours.

Present

Michael Schaal (Chairman)
Chris Booth
Carol Breedon
Kelly Jay
Mike Oates
Judy Prior
Tina Salami
Anne Simpson
Nat Singh
Paul Ure
Jo Van Gyseghem
Brad West
Tam Wyatt
Mel Winters (Secretary)

subject after the meeting.

4 **Business review**

The Chairman presented charts and graphs showing the present position in the Midlands. The Company was 37% below target in the present financial year; the area 19% below. The

reflection of the country's present economic position..

5 **Targets**

Tam Wyatt circulated copies of the February sales targets results. The Chairman congratulated Tina Salami on achieving top sales and said that she had become a valuable member

there would be a promotion on the Golden bar range offeing a 10p money-back coupon on next purchase.

Sales promotional materials, samples and dump bins were provided for sales people to collect at the meeting

7 **Visits**

21.4 Creating frames

Frames are the method through which most graphics features are achieved in Word for Windows. If you have completed Unit 20, you will already have used frames with the Equation Editor and Graph embedded applications.

1 Select the **Frame** button from the toolbar or select **Frame** from the **Insert** menu. The cursor will change to a crosshair.

2 Position the crosshair at the top left corner of the frame position and hold down the left mouse button.

3 Drag the box which is displayed to the size you want and release the mouse button. The frame will be displayed in outline.

1 Load up the file **UNIT21-1.DOC**, if it is not already on screen
2 With the cursor at the position in the file where the 4-column format begins, create a frame 0.5" (1.3 cm) high across the first 2 columns
3 Save the file for further use

21.5 Using frames for text

You can place text in a specified position on the page by putting it in a frame.

1 With the cursor at the position where the text is needed, create a frame.

2 Click the cursor inside the frame.

3 Key in the text and apply a style to it.

Activity 4

1 Load up the file **UNIT21-1.DOC**

2 Create a frame, a distance of 3" (7.6 cm) from the top of the page, across the first 2 columns

3 Enter the text **Column Title** into the frame, emboldening, centring and enlarging the text to 18 point

4 Save and print

Minutes of a meeting of Midlands Sales Staff at Soar House, New Road, Leicester, on 12 March 19xx, at 1000 hours.

Present	**4 Business review**	**5 Targets**	there would be a promotion on the Golden bar range
Michael Schaal (Chairman) Chris Booth Carol Breedon Kelly Jay Mike Oates Judy Prior Tina Salami Anne Simpson Nat Singh Paul Ure Jo Van Gyseghem Brad West Tam Wyatt	The Chairman presented charts and graphs showing the present position in the Midlands. The Company was 37% below target in the present financial year; the area 19% below. The	Tam Wyatt circulated copies of the February sales targets results. The Chairman congratulated Tina Salami on achieving top sales and said that she had become a valuable member	offeing a 10p money-back coupon on next purchase. Sales promotional materials, samples and dump bins were provided for sales people to collect at the meeting

Column Title   7 **Visits**

Important   If you are not happy with the frame you have created, you can delete it and start again or, more usefully, you can edit it to make any amendments you want. This is particularly useful if you merely want to move the box slightly, to change its size or shape, or to edit the text within it.

21.6 Editing frames

1 Select the frame by clicking the pointer slightly to its left. Change its size by dragging its corners or its position by dragging the whole box with the pointer inside it.

2 Select **Frame** from the **Format** menu to display the **Frame** dialog box.

3 Check the position and any features you wish to change for the frame, eg you may want the ordinary text to be a certain distance away from the border.

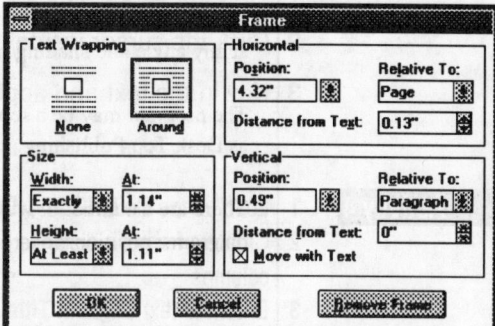

4 If you want the frame an exact size and at an exact position on screen, you must make sure the **Move with Text** radio button is **not** checked. Click on **OK**.

Activity 5

1 Open the file **UNIT21-1.DOC**, if it is not already on screen
2 Increase the size of the heading to 14 point and embolden
3 Move the frame which contains the text **Column Title** to a position 5" (13 cm) from the top of the page, across the middle 2 columns and make it 0.5" (1.3 cm) high
4 Change the text to **This is a liftout** and enlarge it to 24 point
5 Save and print

Minutes of a meeting of Midlands Sales Staff at Soar House, New Road, Leicester, on 12 March 19xx, at 1000 hours.

Present

Michael Schaal (Chairman)
Chris Booth
Carol Breedon
Kelly Jay
Mike Oates
Judy Prior
Tina Salami
Anne Simpson
Nat Singh
Paul Ure
Jo Van Gyseghem
Brad West
Tam Wyatt

4   **Business review**

The Chairman presented charts and graphs showing the present position in the Midlands. The Company was 37% below target in the present financial year; the area 19% below. The

5   **Targets**

Tam Wyatt circulated copies of the February sales targets results. The Chairman congratulated Tina Salami on achieving top sales and said that she had become a valuable member there would be a promotion on the

Golden bar range offeing a 10p money-back coupon on next purchase.

Sales promotional materials, samples and dump bins were provided for sales people to collect at the meeting

7   **Visits**

This is a liftout

1   Clear the screen, if necessary, and key in the text given below, following the display
2   Proofread on screen, spell check and save as file **UNIT21-2.DOC**

Most drawing programs are capable of the following: text in several sizes, weights and styles; simple shapes, such as rectangles, circles and arcs; lines of different thicknesses at any angle and shading in various weights or patterns.

The program may be a separate package or part of a more comprehensive package, such as Desk Top Publishing.

There are a number of ways in which drawing packages can be used, producing simple diagrams; positioning large text on a page and for simple drawings.

Pie chart

A single pie chart can be used to present only *one* set of figures. Each figure is shown as a percentage of the total of all the figures, with the angle of each *pie slice* representing the percentage. It is only suitable for situations when the total is significant; in any other situation, a pie chart will be inappropriate and will give false information.

Bar chart

A bar chart uses the length of bars of equal width to represent one set of numerical values. It enables comparison between the values in the set, merely by looking at the lengths.

Multiple bar chart

If you have more than one set of figures, and comparisons are to be made between sets, as well as between figures in the same set, then multiple bar charts are used. The bars can be *stacked*, ie the second set on top of the first set, in which case the total of the two sets can also be compared. Alternatively, the bars can be next to each other, in which case shading is used to pick out each set of figures.

Line graph

If you are mainly interested in the *change* in one or more set of figures, then a line graph may be suitable, where points are plotted and joined with lines, using different colours or point styles to differentiate between them. Line graphs are most commonly used for changes over time.

Labelling graphs

It is essential to label graphs properly; otherwise anyone using them will not be able to get all the information from them. You should label axes and provide a key to the lines or bars.

1 Load up the file **UNIT21-2.DOC**, if it is not already on screen
2 Set page size to A5 portrait (*see* Unit 12). Set top margin to 0.75" (2 cm) and bottom margin to 0.5" (1.3 cm)
3 Define a two column layout, with margins of 0.5" (1.3 cm) at each side and 0.5" (1.3 cm) between the columns
4 Save the file before continuing
5 Set up 3 styles called Side heading, Sub heading and Main title as follows:
      Side heading - Sans Serif 12 pt, bold, left justified
      Sub heading - Sans Serif 14 pt, bold, centred
      Main title - Sans Serif 18 pt, bold, centred
6 Set the initial font Serif 10 pt, fully justified
7 Apply the style Side heading to each of the headings *Pie chart*, *Bar chart*, etc, as shown in the example
8 Save the file before continuing
9 Add a vertical line between the columns
10 Create a frame across both columns at the top of the page to hold the main title
11 Add a thick horizontal ruling line above the main title
12 Save again and print a copy for reference

Graphics drawing program

Most drawing programs are capable of the following: text in several sizes, weights and styles; simple shapes, such as rectangles, circles and arcs; lines of different thicknesses at any angle and shading in various weights or patterns.

The program may be a separate package or part of a more comprehensive package, such as Desk Top Publishing.

There are a number of ways in which drawing packages can be used, producing simple diagrams; positioning large text on a page and for simple drawings.

Pie chart

A single pie chart can be used to present only *one* set of figures. Each figure is shown as a percentage of the total of all the figures, with the angle of each *pie slice* representing the percentage. It is only suitable for situations when the total is significant; in any other situation, a pie chart will be inappropriate and will give false information.

Bar chart

A bar chart uses the length of bars of equal width to represent one set of numerical values. It enables comparison between the values in the set, merely by looking at the lengths.

Multiple bar chart

If you have more than one set of figures, and comparisons are to be made between sets, as well as between figures in the same set, then multiple bar charts are used. The bars can be *stacked*, ie the second set on top of the first set, in which case the total of the two sets can also be compared. Alternatively, the bars can be next to each other, in

21.7 Creating drawings

You may want to create and display simple drawings. With the built in **Draw** application, you can create rectangles, ellipses, circles, arcs, lines and text in black and white and colours (less useful without a colour printer). A drawing is treated as an object, just like an equation or a graph.

1 Select the **Draw** button from the toolbar or select **Object** from the **Insert** menu, followed by **Microsoft Drawing** to load the built in **Draw** application.

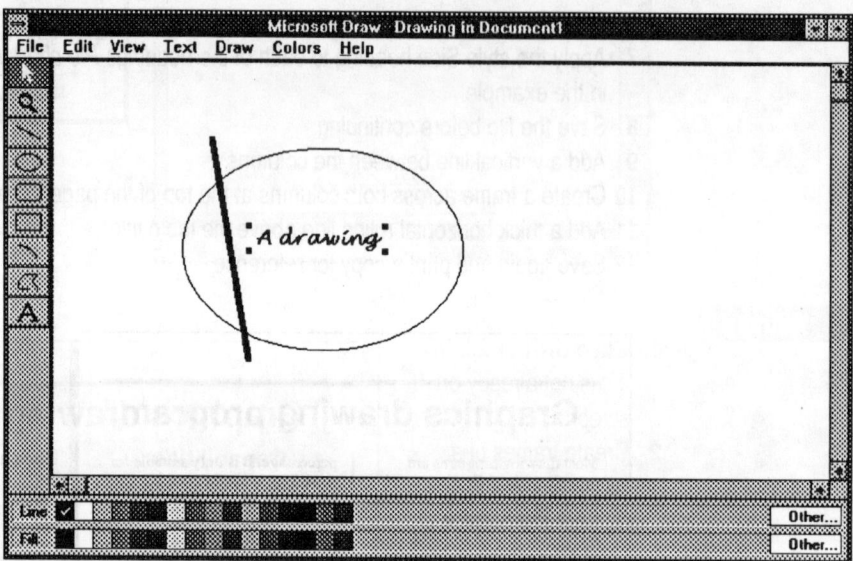

2 Click on the shape you want from the toolbar at the left of the screen. Choose a colour from the palette at the bottom for lines and fills (closed shapes only).

3 Click on the arrow tool to select objects, move them, change their size, line thickness or fill. You can also Copy and Paste objects, or groups of objects, as in the pattern shown on the right, which is made up of copied rectangles with square and rounded corners.

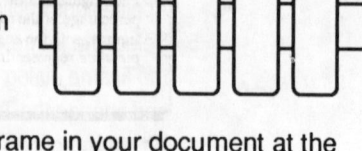

4 Select **Exit and Return to Filename** from the **File** menu to return to your text. A dialog box will be displayed.

5 Select **OK** to put the new drawing into a frame in your document at the cursor position.

Activity 7

1 Open the file **UNIT21-2.DOC**, if it is not already on screen
2 Position the cursor in the first column
3 Create the simple drawing shown below, using the ellipse/circle tool, selecting the object and then applying a white line and a grey fill.
4 Select **Other** for fill to display the **Other Colour** dialog box and click on a lighter shade of grey
5 Click **OK** to confirm, then save the drawing

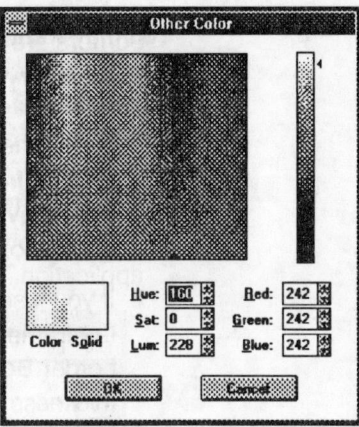

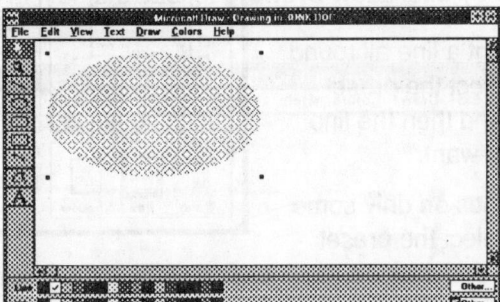

Activity 8

1 Open **UNIT21-2.DOC**, if it is not already on screen
2 Create frames of a suitable size and in the appropriate positions to act as headings in a column, for each of the sub headings shown in the sample, eg Capabilities
3 Apply the Sub heading style to each of the new headings
4 Position the drawing created in Activity 7 so as to shade the Applications section
5 Select the frame, display the **Frame** dialog box and change the **Text Wrapping** option to **None**, so that it is displayed over the text
6 Save and print a copy

Graphics drawing program

Capabilities

Most drawing programs are capable of the following: text in several sizes, weights and styles; simple shapes, such as rectangles, circles and arcs; lines of different thicknesses at any angle and shading in various weights or patterns. The program may be a separate package or part of a more comprehensive package, such as Desk Top Publishing.

Applications

There are a number of ways in which drawing packages can be used, prod̶ ̶ ̶ ̶ ̶ ̶ ̶ ̶ms; posit̶ ̶ ̶ ̶ ̶ ̶ ̶ ̶ ̶d for̶ ̶ ̶ ̶ ̶ ̶ ̶

Pi̶ ̶

A single p̶ ̶ ̶ ̶ ̶ ̶ ̶ ̶ to present only one set of figures. Each figure is shown as a percentage of the total of all the figures, with the angle of each pie slice representing the percentage. It is only suitable for situations when the total is significant; in any other situation, a pie chart will be inappropriate and will give false information.

Bar chart

A bar chart uses the length of bars of equal width to represent one set of numerical values. It enables comparison between the values in the set, merely by looking at the lengths.

Multiple bar chart

If you have more than one set of figures, and comparisons are to be made between sets, as well as between figures in the same set, then multiple bar charts are used. The bars can be *stacked*, ie the second set on top of the first set, in which case the total of the two sets can also be compared. Alternatively, the bars can be next to each other, in which case shading is used to pick out each set of figures.

Line graph

If you are mainly interested in the *change* in one or more set of figures, then a line graph may be suitable, where points are plotted and joined with lines, using different colours or point styles to differentiate between them. Line graphs are most commonly used for changes over time.

21.8 Adding borders to frames

Borders are added to frames in exactly the same way as for tables or text, using a very similar dialog box.

1 Select the frame, then select **Border** from the **Format** menu to display the **Border Picture** dialog box.

2 If you just want a line all round the frame, select the preset border **Box** and then the line thickness you want.

3 If you want lines on only some sides, then select the preset border **None** and click on the lines you want in the diagram.

4 Click **OK** to return to the text. The frame will now have borders.

Activity 8

1 Open the file **UNIT21-2.DOC**, if it is not already on screen
2 With the cursor in suitable positions in the text, create sample graphs for each section, as shown below.
3 Put borders round each graph and change their sizes to fit the columns, as in the sample
4 Save and print

Pie Chart with legend and data labels

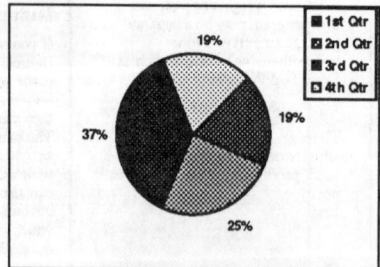

Columns with legend

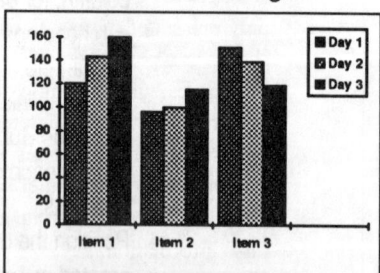

Line with grid

3D Bars with legend

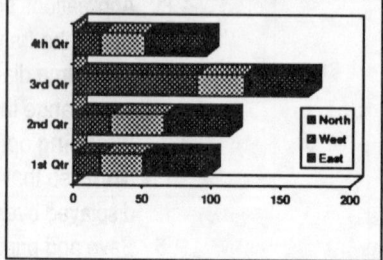

Graphics drawing programs

Capabilities

Most drawing programs are capable of the following: text in several sizes, weights and styles; simple shapes, such as rectangles, circles and arcs; lines of different thicknesses at any angle and shading in various weights or patterns. The program may be a separate package or part of a more comprehensive package, such as Desk Top Publishing.

s.   n
a pag

Choosing graphics

Pie chart

A single pie chart can be used to present only one set of figures. Each figure is shown as a percentage of the total of all the figures, with the angle of each pie slice representing the percentage. It is only suitable for situations when the total is significant; in any other situation, a pie chart will be inappropriate and will give false information.

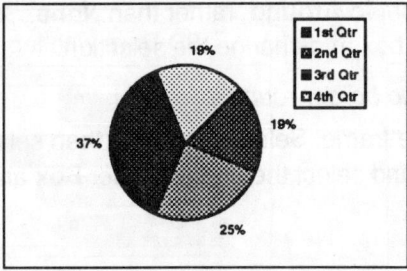

Bar chart

A bar chart uses the length of bars of equal width to represent one set of numerical values. It enables comparison between the values in the set, merely by looking at the lengths.

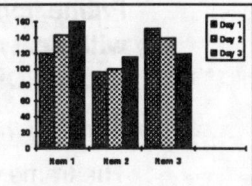

Multiple bar chart

If you have more than one set of figures, and comparisons are to made between sets, as well as between figures in the same set, then multiple bar charts are used. The bars can be stacked, ie the second set on top of the first set, in which case the total of the two sets

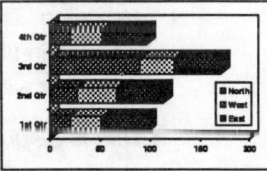

can also be compared. Alternatively, the bars can be next to each other, in which case shading is used to pick out each set of figures.

Line graph

If you are mainly interested in the change in one or more sets of figures, then a

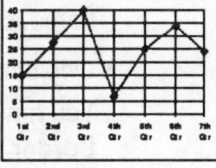

line graph may be suitable, where points

1 Concert programmes

2 Magazines

3 Brochures

• *One of the graph or drawing frames you created is not in the position on the page you intended.*

The frame is moving with the text to keep in the same cursor position relative to your text from when you created it. Select the frame and select **Frame** from the **Format** menu to display the **Frame** dialog box. If the **Move with Text** radio button is checked, then click on it to remove the check. Click on **OK**. You should then be able to reposition the frame as you choose.

• *Some of the body text is beside the sub headings.*

The frame you created to hold the sub heading was not as wide as the column, so text wrapped round it. Adjust the frame to fit the exact width of the column. The text will be moved to its correct position.

• *You cannot see the columns displayed on screen.*

You have selected normal display, rather than Page Layout. Display the **View** menu and select **Page Layout**. The columns should now be displayed.

• *The headings and text are not in the same positions on the page as in the sample.*

The exact display and line endings will depend on the fonts and printer you are using. The sample page is printed on an Apple Laserwriter IINT using the built in Helvetica font. Your sans serif font may have quite different character widths.

• *Text is displayed over one or more of the graph frames.*

The frame has **Text Wrapping** set to **None**, rather than **Around**. Select the frame, display the **Frame** dialog box and change the selection.

• *The shaded ellipse drawing is not displayed over the Applications section; it is on its own.*

The frame has **Text Wrapping** set to **Around**, rather than **None**. Select the frame, display the **Frame** dialog box and change the selection.

• *One or more graph frames has no border round it.*

You have not set a border for the frame. Select the frame, then select **Border** from the **Format** menu and select the preset border **Box** and a suitable line width.

Glossary

Align	To place text in a straight line, either to the left or to the right
Block	A piece of text which has been marked by selecting Block from the Edit menu or by using the mouse
Backspace delete	Key which deletes the character to the left of the cursor
Break	Ending a page or column before its default position
Bullet	Circle or other character used to emphasise items in a list
Button	A screen icon which gives quick access to an operation or dialog box
Calculations	A facility within tables which allows manipulation of numbers
Centring	Positioning text centrally on a line
Close	Remove a file from the screen and save it to disk, if necessary
Cursor	A flashing video block marking the point where text is entered
Cut and paste	Remove blocks of text or move them to a new position
Date code	Facility allowing the current date to be inserted into your document
Default	Any pre-set value, for margins, tabs, paper size, printer, font, alignment or any other feature
Delete	Key which deletes the character at the cursor position
Dialog box	A box displayed on screen which gives a range of options to the user for a particular operation
Draw application	Embedded application used to create drawings

Editing	Making changes by deleting, inserting or moving text
Edit menu	Menu containing all editing and movement options
Embolden	Enhance text to give a darker, thicker effect
Enhancement	Emboldening, underlining, italics and other effects used to highlight or enhance text
Equation editor	Embedded application used to create equations
Field	An item of data contained in a record
File menu	Menu for file, printing and setup operations
Font	A style of print. A font list is given in the Font menu
Font menu	Menu containing all font and appearance options
Footer	A line of text which appears on all or alternate pages containing file names and page numbers
Footnote	An addition to an item in the text, placed at the bottom of the appropriate page, or the end of the document
Format	The layout of a document or file
Format menu	Menu for all layout commands, including page, paragraph, character and border characteristics and styles
Formulae	Mathematical computations in tables
Frame	Defined rectangular area which can contain text, equations, graphs, drawings or imported graphics
Global replace	Replacement of text which is carried out automatically for every occurrence of the text
Graph application	Embedded application used to create graphs
Hard copy	A paper copy of the work on screen
Header	A line of text appearing on all or alternate pages
Highlight	Reverse video shading, or colour, which can help you to identify text to be changed or moved
Horizontal centring	Work centred across a page
Indent	Text inset from the main body of the work
Initial Codes	The default codes for a document
Inserting rows/cols	Adding rows and columns to a table
Insert mode	Keying text inserts it before the existing text
Insert menu	Menu containing all special features which can be inserted into a document, including objects

Installation	Setting up your software program for use on your particular equipment
Joining/merging cells	The Tables facility which allows cell manipulation to allow for long titles
Justify	Text with an even left or right margin
Macro	Standard operations composed by selecting Macro from the Tools menu
Mailmerge	Merging 2 files to produce a personalised letter
Move	A function to move or cut text through the Edit menu
Menu bar	The top line of the screen which contains all the main menu options
Numbering	Button on ribbon giving automatic numbering of points
On line	An active operation, particularly an active printer
Open	Retrieve a previously saved file from disk and display it on screen
Outlining	A system of numbering automatically and organising text hierarchically
Pagination	This is the way in which pages are organised and numbered
Page break	Ending a page at a specified point
Paper size	A set size and type of paper used for printing
Paste	Place text which has been cut in a new position
Preview	Inspect the layout of your document before printing
Record	Data stored for reference purposes
Retrieve	Recall a file from disk for editing or subsequent use
Ribbon	Horizontal portion of screen containing the buttons used for formatting text, eg Bold, Numbering
Right align	Line text up to the right margin, or to a set point on the page
Ruler	Horizontal screen marker showing margins, tabs and measurements currently in use
Ruling lines	Horizontal and vertical lines used to emphasise text or items

Selective replace	Replacement of text which has to be confirmed for every occurrence of the text
Setup	Menu option which lets you choose display, editing, hardware and menu options
Spell check	Looking up words in a disk-based dictionary to find and correct spelling and typing mistakes
Style	A set of features specifying the appearance of text
Subscript	Smaller lowered character
Superscript	Smaller raised characters
Tab key	Key providing automatic stops for text insertion at intervals
Table	A method of displaying text in columns and rows, which can be used in preference to tab settings
Table menu	Menu containing all the options needed for table use
Template	File containing a standard document, which can be used to produce this sort of document
Text size	The text sizes you can use depend on the printer you are using. To view the sizes available, print out the file PRINTER.TST
Thesaurus	A method of looking up alternative words
Toolbar	Portion of screen containing buttons which give quick access to menu options
Tools menu	Menu containing special options, eg Spellcheck, Thesaurus, macros, mailmerge
Typing screen	The screen that you see; it usually contains 22 lines
Undelete	If you have deleted a line and then changed your mind, you may undelete through the Edit menu
Underline	One of the ways in which the appearance of text can be altered, found in the Font menu, or using key **F8**
View menu	Menu allowing a variety of different views of the document on which you are working
Window menu	Menu showing all the currently open files from which other files can be chosen for display

Index